Is Critique Secular?
Blasphemy, Injury, and Free Speech

THE TOWNSEND PAPERS IN THE HUMANITIES *No. 2*

Is Critique Secular?
Blasphemy, Injury, and Free Speech

Talal Asad

Wendy Brown

Judith Butler

Saba Mahmood

Published by
The Townsend Center for the Humanities
University of California | Berkeley

Distributed by
University of California Press
Berkeley, Los Angeles, London | 2009

ISBN 978-0-9823294-1-2

Library of Congress Cataloging-in-Publication Data

Is critique secular? blasphemy, injury, and free speech/Talal Asad...[et al.].
     p. cm. — (The Townsend papers in the humanities; no.2)
ISBN 978-0-9823294-1-2
1. Freedom of speech. 2. Blasphemy (Islam) 3. Islam and secularism.
I. Asad, Talal.
 JC591.I73 2009
 323.44'3091767—dc22

                          2009033961

Inquiries concerning proposals for the Townsend Papers in the Humanities
from Berkeley faculty and Townsend Center affiliates should be addressed to
The Townsend Papers, 220 Stephens Hall, UC Berkeley, Berkeley, CA 94720-
2340, or by email to townsend_papers@lists.berkeley.edu

Design and typesetting: Kajun Graphics

Manufactured in the United States of America

Table of Contents

Wendy Brown

Introduction

THE ESSAYS COMPRISING this volume were first presented at a fall 2007 symposium, "Is Critique Secular?" sponsored by the Townsend Center for the Humanities at the University of California, Berkeley.[1] The symposium was conceived as the inaugural public event for a new research and teaching program in critical theory at Berkeley, a program that aims to bridge conventional divides between modern European critical theory and non-Western and post-Enlightenment critical theoretical projects. A symposium probing the presumed secularism of critique seemed an especially promising way to launch a program with such ambitions.

While the symposium papers addressed a variety of topics, the publication of those by Talal Asad and Saba Mahmood seemed useful because their analyses focused on the Danish cartoon affair—the protests and debates surrounding the 2005 Danish newspaper publication of a series of cartoons satirizing the Prophet Muhammad. Insofar as this affair raised a nest of (often unasked) questions about conventional ordinances of secularity, religion, insult, injury, blasphemy, free speech, dissent, and criticism, it provided an extraordinary platform for rethinking the putatively secular foundations and premises of critique.

This introduction commences with the opening remarks I made at the symposium itself. It then offers a brief orientation to the essays published here.

Is Critique Secular?

The question, is critique secular? would seem to imitate critique's direct interrogative modality and secularism's putative transparency, conveying as well an expectation of rational consideration conventionally associated with both critique and secularism. The directness and transparency evaporate, of course, the moment the terms of the title are closely scrutinized. Indeed, the question invites its own dispersion, dissemination, disorientation. It invites, in other words, the work of critique. Those who posed the question, the conference organizers, knew its terms would not stay still and are among the scholars who have problematized such terms extensively in their own work. But they knew as well that the Western academy is governed by the presumptive secularism of critique, and that it is with this governance that we must begin. Unseating governance of this sort is the very signature of political, social, and cultural critique; it targets what is presumptive, sure, commonsensical, or given in the current order of things.

It may be helpful briefly to query the relation between the patently unfixed quality of the terms of the question, is critique secular? and the historical force of the impulse to fix each and bind them together. To this end, let us make each term wobble a bit and then consider what secures them so tightly to one another.

Is . . .

After Bill Clinton's infamous account of why he had not exactly lied in denying a sexual relationship with Monica Lewinsky—"[I]t depends on what the meaning of the word, 'is' is"—the sliding signification of this tiny but potent verb is seared in the popular imagination and not only the erudite one. And Clinton was on to something. "Is" can be temporal (setting the present off from past and future) or ontological; it can refer to essence or existence; it can be performative or constative; it can be mobilized to insist, declare, refute, or simply posit. And placed as an interrogative, it inverts its power of fixity and certainty; it undoes itself.

Critique . . .

From Reinhart Kosellek's *Critique and Crisis*, we learn that critique emerges in ancient Athens as the jurisprudential term *krisis*.[2] Nearly untranslatable from the holistic Greek context to our much more compartmentalized one, *krisis* integrates polis rupture, tribunal, knowledge, judgment, and repair at the same time that it links subject and object in practice. *Krisis* refers to a specific work of the polis on itself—a practice of sifting, sorting, judging, and repairing what has been rent by a citizen violation of polis law or order. As the term winds its way into Latin and then the vernacular European languages, critique loses this many-faceted holism. It retreats mainly into medical vocabulary where it signifies the turning point in an illness, a usage that persists into the present. However, critique remains distinguished from criticism for much of modernity and especially for Kant and Marx, who distanced themselves respectively from "criticasters," and "critical critics."[3]

Apart from the historical shifts, there is, of course, a world of difference between the meanings of critique thus far identified and those now practiced under the sign of ideology critique, cultural critique, identity critique, and so on. At times today the term is taken to convey polemical rejection, at other times to signal immanent or deconstructive analytic practices, and at still others, to identify the search for a secreted truth within a tissue of mystifications. In all of its uses, however, critique would seem to carry a tacit presumption of reason's capacity to unveil error. Therein lies part of our problem.

Secular?

This term, which issues etymologically from a certain notion of time, has come to stand in commonsense fashion for post-Reformation practices and institutions in the West that formally separate private religious belief (or nonbelief) from public life. Yet it is not only Talal Asad who has dislodged this meaning with his insistence on pluralizing *formations* of the secular (in his book by that title) but also Charles Taylor who, in his history of Christian secularism, backgrounds this meaning to focus on the making of the secular subject and its unique experience of the world.[4] Consider, too, the train of associations with the secular that betray the commonsensical meaning—"secular" can suggest a condition of being unreligious or antireligious, but also religiously tolerant, humanist, Christian, modern, or simply Western. And any effort at settling the term immediately meets its doom in the conflicts among these associations, conflicts epitomized by the recent phenomenon of an American neoconservative political agenda that simultaneously sought to legitimize Christian prayer in American public schools and to make secularization a central tenet of the regime change project in the Middle East. Indeed, today the secular derives much of its meaning from an imagined opposite in Islam, and, as such, veils the religious shape and content of Western public life and its imperial designs. Yet something named "secular humanism" is also targeted by the right in domestic American politics, held responsible by its decriers for destroying the fabrics of the family, the moral individual, and patriotism.

Uncritical Secularism

If secularism and critique slide in so many directions, and are so unfixed in their respective meanings and reach, how did they become thoroughly bound to one another? Indeed, how has critique come to be defined as secular, and how has secularism come to be understood as both what animates critique and what critique yields? Clearly a constellation of Enlightenment conceits is part of what allows critique to comport so readily with secularism: from Mill to Marx, Diderot to Kant and Hume, we greet the Enlightenment presumption that the true, the objective, the real, the rational, and even the scientific emerge only with the shedding of religious authority or "prejudice." This presumption reaches an apex in the Kantian dictum that everything must submit to critique, even reason itself, and also in Hegel's attempt to reveal the rational kernel of Christianity through a critical history and phenomenology. Hence the conviction that critique displaces religious and other unfounded authority and prejudice with reason, even as it may leave religion itself standing. Hence too, the conviction that critique replaces opinion or faith with truth, and subjectivism with science; that critique is, in short, secular.

But even this story does not quite apprehend the intensity with which critique attaches itself to secularism, articulates itself as a secularizing project, and identifies itself with the dethroning of God. For an appreciation of this intensity, we must consider Marx's own development of critique out of what he took to be the shortcomings of the Young Hegelians' critical approach to religion. Bruno Bauer, Max Stirner and others criticized religion as illusory consciousness that obscured the real and the true about human powers and human existence. Initially caught up in this project, Marx soon turned against it, and did so by distinguishing criticism, "mere criticism" or "critical criticism," from critique. This is the move that really secures the conviction that critique is secular in the Western critical theory tradition. How does it go?

Marx's objection to the Young Hegelians was that they regarded criticism of religious illusion as the road to freedom. For them, if both man and the state shed religious for rational consciousness, both would be freed from error, partiality, and particularity and hence would be free as such. Marx took a different approach. Drawing on, yet transforming, Ludwig Feuerbach's critique of religion, Marx regarded religious consciousness not merely as error but as existing for a reason and, above all, as the symptom of unhappy and unfree human existence. The very fact of religious consciousness was the sign of an unfree world, a world that "requires illusion." Thus, God is "the illusory sun about which man revolves so long as he does not revolve around himself," something he cannot do until his existence is emancipated.[5] For Marx, then, there was a great difference between criticism of religion as illusory and *a critique* of the *conditions* that produce religious consciousness and that religion can be seen to express. Mere criticism marks religion as false; critique connects religious illusions, and the need for them, to the specific reality generating and necessitating religious consciousness. In addition, critique discerns in religion the desire for a different world, one in which we all are "equal in the eyes of god," in which "the meek shall inherit the earth," or in which the powers and virtues previously conferred to a divinity are finally known and lived as human powers. So critique not only links religion to historical conditions of unfreedom but also reads religion as indirectly harboring the wishes and aspirations of humanity against its suffering in the present. Religion is both "the expression of... suffering and a protest against it."[6]

What has happened here? Marx has founded his distinction between criticism and critique in the latter's ability to (1) apprehend the real order of things, (2) explain why this real order is not manifest but requires critique to be revealed, and (3) explain what kind of human future is adumbrated in religious illusion. Critique is premised upon a historically necessary mystification of reality, a mystification required by the unfree, inegalitarian, and unhappy nature of existence, and it promises to scientifically decode that mystification. Thus Marx brings together in the notion of critique a comprehension of the Real identified as the material, a practice of objectivity identified with science, and the realization of true emancipation of religion, true secularism, in place of what he decries as "merely theological criticism" (where secularism stands both for the unreligious and also, as Charles Taylor would have it, the capacity to live to one side of one's milieu, to grasp its contingency rather than simply be steeped in it).

It is this particular heritage from Marx, and the way it threads through German critical theory right up through Habermas, that has so overdetermined the imbrication, indeed the identification, of critique with secularism in the tradition of Western critical theory. Within this tradition, critique has for more than 150 years been bound to an apprehension of a set of human arrangements that generate religious illusion, even when religion is not the express target of critique. Critique in this tradition has prided itself on explaining both mystifications and human consort with these mystifications from a place imagined to be their opposite in every respect. Thus does the rational, material, real, scientific, and human aim both to explain and supplant the religious, the ideal, the unreal, the speculative, and the divine.

So it is no small thing this symposium does in posing the question, is critique secular? Far more than asking after varieties of critique or varieties of secularism, this question upends one of critical theory's founding planks. Yet it does so in a spirit that allows for the possibility of other formulations of critique, secularism, and their relation. These formulations might loosen critique's identity with secularism as well as surrender its reliance on a notion of secularism itself insulated from critique.

The question, is critique secular? is also posed at a political-historical juncture when intellectuals face something of a choice between complicity with imperial and unreflexive Western civilizational discourses of rationality and secularism on the one hand, and with challenging Western presumptions to monopolize the fact, meaning, and content of secularism, rationalism, freedom, and even democracy on the other. If, as Talal Asad suggests in this volume, the Western civilizational identity rooted in a presumed convergence of Christianity, secularism, liberalism, democracy, and liberty is opened up, Westerners might begin to think differently about themselves and their imagined global opposites. So there is both a theoretical and political incitement for the inquiry this symposium inaugurates, a combination that itself heralds the work of critique.

"FREE SPEECH, BLASPHEMY, AND SECULAR CRITICISM," Talal Asad's erudite and indirect critique of received Western understandings of critique, performs rhetorically what it calls for explicitly. Rather than pressing a linear logical analytics, it interrupts at every turn a set of discursive oppositions between Islam and secular Christianity on issues of freedom, speech, and blasphemy, and between a political Islam identified with aggression and death and a secular West identified with rationality and life. Asad has long resisted attempts to define the secular and the religious and has shown them rather to be interdependent and fluctuating notions constituting a crucial domain of modern power and governance. Thus the status of belief and blasphemy alter in relation to the powers of the modern state and are, among other things, effects of expansions and changes in these powers.

Asad's starting point is the Danish cartoon controversy, in which twelve editorial cartoons viciously satirizing the Prophet Muhammad were published in a Danish newspaper in 2005 and then republished by several European newspapers in 2008. The cartoons were greeted by most religious Muslims as insulting, violent, and/or blasphemous, and the publications incited rage and protest from Muslims around the world.

Through close consideration of the problematic of blasphemy, Asad begins undoing the discursive-intellectual binary that lines up Christianity, secularism, reason, tolerance, free thought and speech on one side, and Islam, fundamentalism, submission, intolerance, restricted thought and speech on the other. This in turn allows him to challenge a more specific antinomy between secular criticism and religious censure, in which the former is associated with freedom, truth, and reason and the latter with intolerance, obscurantism, arbitrary dictum, and coercion. Within these binary orders, the very existence of the crime of blasphemy in Islamic society suggests to Western ears the absence of free speech (and by implication the absence of freedom *tout court*). But this is only so, Asad argues, because of a Western conceit of the self-owning individual presumed free from all forms of coercion, including those potentially entailed in religion, commerce, love, belief, and comportment.

Asad contests this conceit as a matter of simple fact—reminding us of the daily coercions exercised by the inarticulate powers coursing through liberal orders—but also suggests that it meets its own limits in a variety of express concerns within liberal societies, including one shared with Islam: the problem of seduction, and its cousin, moral corruption. It is along this trail that Asad is able to reveal to liberal subjects that they are not quite so self-owning as official discourse suggests, and that concerns with "blasphemy" as a violent breaking of constraints is as present in putatively secular societies as it is in overtly theocratic ones, even if framed through a different vocabulary and living below the political surface of liberal orders. The modern Western opposition between freedom and blasphemy permits Westerners to believe that they are free of the restrictions a discourse of blasphemy imposes, while denying the belonging to a particular way of life that secularism must protect in other, less forthrightly religious terms.

Above all, Asad's essay reveals how different conceptualizations of belief, freedom, and truth produce different possibilities *for action* in the world. If, as in one strand of Christianity, the "truth shall set you free," and freedom is understood as the removal of constraints, then freedom of speech is a first principle of both truth and freedom. But if, as in certain practices of Islam, individual belief is considered inscrutable by any being other than God, what matters is not individual belief but rather social practices and public behaviors. Within Islam, belief is not a space of indemnity but is, rather, inscrutable. Belief's relation to freedom in Islam is thus very different from that which is featured in a Christian trajectory of blasphemy and free speech.

Through this framing, Asad can then provide depth and immediacy to two contemporary questions: "Does the modern liberal aversion to the category of blasphemy derive from a suspicion of political religion?" and, "Why is it that aggression in the name of God shocks secular liberal sensibilities, whereas the act of killing in the name of the secular nation, or of democracy, does not?" While the analysis he has developed to this point identifies the logical fallacies and hypocrisies of these conundrums, Asad is uninterested in such analytics. Instead, he leaves us with a devastating open-ended reflection on the investments and affect of (Western) paranoia.

In "Religious Reason and Secular Affect," Saba Mahmood also begins with the Danish cartoons but turns from a presumed clash between blasphemy and free speech probed so productively by Asad to interrogate a different dimension of the religiously based presumptions and affect of Euro-Atlantic secularism. For Mahmood, the Christian secular understanding of blasphemy cannot fathom the violence or moral injury that the cartoons cause to believing Muslims. This is because of significant differences in what she calls "reading practices" flowing from Islamic piety (a tradition of interpretation that is challenged by many Muslims) and secular Protestantism and, more precisely, different semiotics of iconography and representation especially pertinent to religious deities and prophets. Importantly, these are semiotic differences—not oppositions and not developmental intervals in which, for example, Christianity represents a modernist achievement at which Islam has not yet arrived. In other words, if Protestant Christians know that religious signs "are not embodiments of the divine but only stand in for it through an act of human coding and interpretation," while Islamic pietists experience the negative iconography in the cartoons as a direct assault, this is not due to a hermeneutic sophistication of the former over the latter. Rather, it is because Protestant Christianity figures religious authority as distant and command-based, while for Islamic pietists one "ingest[s], as it were, the Prophet's persona," emulating "how he dressed…ate… spoke to his friends and adversaries…slept, walked, and so on."[7] Thus an attack on the Prophet's persona, such as the satires featured in the cartoons, does not merely defile him but constitutes a direct assault on his followers.

Mahmood is *not* arguing that this difference is an inherent one between Islam and Christianity but, rather, that it pertains to a particular (and contestable) modality of belief and hermeneutics in certain traditions within each religion. Without an appreciation of this difference, the offence and injury that the cartoons caused for many remained unarticulated and unrecognized; the debates remained locked in an unreflexive and one-sided hermeneutic taken to be the only hermeneutic.

The implications of this difference comprise only one part of Mahmood's account of how the Danish cartoon episode was cast within a European Christian worldview that anoints itself as secular. Also important is the way this casting at once racialized Muslims and denied such racialization, a casting that permitted the insistence that religion rather than race was being satirized in the cartoons. (Had race been considered to be at issue, various national and European Court hate speech laws would have kicked in to censor the publication and circulation of the cartoons.) Despite Europe's own exceptionally confused and confusing history on the distinction and fusions of race and religion—a history that features, *inter alia*, the racialization of Aryans, Jews, Roma, and northern Irish Protestants and Catholics—most Europeans engaging the Danish cartoon affair insisted on a pure and purely religious categorization of Islam, casting religion as a "choice" rather than an ascriptive or biological identity. But the conceit of religion as a matter of individual choice, Mahmood reminds us, is already a distinct (and distinctly Protestant) way of conceiving of religion, one that is woefully inapt for Islam and, I might add, for Judaism, which is why neither comports easily with the privatized individual religious subject presumed by the formulations of religious freedom and tolerance governing Euro-Atlantic modernity.

In Judith Butler's response to the essays by Asad and Mahmood, she weaves together and extends their critiques of the inherent secularism imputed to critique in the modern Western tradition. Butler affirms their challenges to Western representations of blasphemy, injury, and freedom by underscoring the fact that there is always a normative framework constraining and regulating the semantic fields in which such terms operate. But not only do normative frameworks constrain the fields, they animate our critical perspectives too, that is, our critiques of these fields are themselves driven by normative commitments that aim to remake our affective and moral responses to the world we inhabit. Butler also returns to the notion of critique itself, not only to reestablish its distinction from criticism, but also to formulate it as a rich, embodied practice—one that draws the subject and object of critique into a new relation while avoiding conventional conceits of objectivity. She draws our attention to the ways that both Asad and Mahmood perform this kind of critique in their analyses of the responses to the Dutch cartoon affair, and adds to these considerations her own critique of sexual freedom in "secular" Dutch immigration politics.

If these critiques of secular framings of recent political conflicts in putatively secular polities reveal the limitations of these framings, then they will also have succeeded in opening the questions of whether critique itself is or must be secular, and of whether secularism is the prerequisite of critique. Such openings comprise the modest ambition of this volume.

Endnotes

[1] The organizers of the symposium were Judith Butler, Saba Mahmood, and Cristopher Nealon. The other participants included Amy Hollywood and Colin Jager. For further information on the program, see http://townsendcenter.berkeley.edu/swg_crittheory.shtml.

[2] Reinhart Koselleck, *Critique and Crisis: Enlightenment and the Pathogenesis of Modern Society* (Cambridge, MA, 1988). In Talal Asad's contribution to this volume, he offers a somewhat different etymology of "critique" and "criticism" from that set out here and treats the two terms as French and English equivalents of each other.

[3] Although Paul Krugman once quipped that "any noun can be verbed," the contemporary coinage of "critique" as a verb surely signifies the erosion of its valuable distance from criticism.

[4] Talal Asad, *Formations of the Secular: Christianity, Islam, Modernity* (Palo Alto, 2003); Charles Taylor, *A Secular Age* (Cambridge, 2007).

[5] Karl Marx, "Contribution to the Critique of Hegel's *Philosophy of Right,* Introduction," in *The Marx-Engels Reader,* 2nd ed., ed. R. Tucker (New York, 1978), p. 54.

[6] Ibid., p. 54.

[7] Saba Mahmood, "Religious Reason and Secular Affect: An Incommensurable Divide?" in this volume.

Talal Asad

Free Speech, Blasphemy, and Secular Criticism

FOR MANY YEARS NOW, there has been much talk in Euro-America
about the threat to free speech, particularly whenever its Muslims
have raised the issue of blasphemy in response to some public
criticism of Islam. The most recent crisis was the scandal of the
Danish cartoons.[1] A decade and a half after the Rushdie affair,
the old religious denunciation of "blasphemy" had reared its head
again among Muslims in Europe and beyond, seeking to undermine hard-won secular freedoms. Or so we were told. There were
angry protests and some violence on one side, many affirmations
of principle and expressions of outrage on the other.[2] The affair
was discussed largely in the context of the problem of integrating
Muslim immigrants into European society and how it related to
the "global menace" of Islamists.[3] Coming after the attack on the
World Trade Center and the London bombings, the cartoon scandal was linked to a wider discourse: the West's "War on Terror,"
a conflict that many see as part of an intrinsic hostility between
two civilizations, Islam and Europe. Thus the Danish press and
many Danish politicians began to criticize Islamic studies scholars of Islam for disregarding this fundamental antagonism. It was
argued that these scholars had intentionally avoided certain civi-

lizational topics, such as the ways in which Islam is not only an obstacle to integration but a potential security threat.[4]

The attitudes displayed in the cartoon affair by Muslims and non-Muslims were quite remarkable. However, this essay is neither an apologia for, nor a criticism of, those attitudes; it is an attempt to think about the place of blasphemy—a religious concept—in secular liberal society. In what follows I want to think about blasphemy from various angles and treat it as the crystallization of some moral and political problems in liberal Europe. So I will have less to say about traditions of Islamic thought and behavior than about the modern secular condition we all inhabit.

Blasphemy as a Sign of Civilizational Identity

The conflict that many Euro-Americans saw in the Danish cartoons scandal was between the West and Islam, each championing opposing values: democracy, secularism, liberty, and reason on one side, and on the other the many opposites—tyranny, religion, authority, and violence. The idea of blasphemy clearly belongs to the latter series and is seen by secularists as a constraint on the freedom of speech—on freedom itself—guaranteed by democratic principles and by the pursuit of reason so central to Western culture. Pope Benedict's Regensburg lecture in 2006 emphasized the idea of a civilizational confrontation between *Christianity*, which reconciles Greek reason with biblical faith, and *Islam*, which encourages violent conversion because it has no faith in reason.[5]

Free speech, it is said, is central to democracy. Consistent with the standpoint of Pope Benedict and many of the defenders of the Danish cartoons, it is often claimed that democracy is rooted in Christianity and is therefore alien to Islam. There is a widespread conviction that Christian doctrine has been receptive to democracy because in Christendom (unlike Islam) church and state began as separate entities. The notion of historical origins is more problematic than is popularly supposed: when did Christianity begin? Or Islam? It must not be forgotten that the Byzantine state-church was the space in which central Christian doctrines were formulated and fought over, that even in the Middle Ages and well beyond, the separation between religious and political authority was far from complete, and that political inequality was generally regarded as legitimate. This is not to say that all those who sought to maintain inequality were Christian and that their opponents were always non-Christian. As all historians of the subject know, the struggle for equal rights was ideologically and socially complicated.

Many Euro-Americans, including, most recently, Francis Fukuyama, have traced "democracy" through "political equality" to the Christian doctrine of "the universal dignity of man," in order to make the claim that it is a unique value of Western civilization.[6] In Medieval Latin, however, *dignitas* was used to refer to the privilege and distinction of high office, not to the equality of all human beings. Christianity does have a notion of universal spiritual worth (as, for that matter, does Islam), but that has been compatible with great social and political inequality. In the nineteenth century some writers (for example, the very influential George Grote) began to trace the concept and practice of modern democracy not from Christianity but from classical Greece.[7] Pre-Christian Athens certainly had a concept of equal, albeit restricted, citizenship and rudimentary democratic practices, which included the right to speak freely in the political forum, but it had no notion of "the universal dignity of man." In European Christendom it was only gradually, through continuous conflict, that many inequalities were eliminated and that secular authority replaced one that was ecclesiastical.

There is a story told by writers of whom Marcel Gauchet is a much-cited example:[8] Christianity is the seed that flowers into secular humanism, destroying in the process its own transcendental orientation and making possible the terrestrial autonomy that now lies at the heart of Western democratic society. (This contrasts with Muslim societies, which remain mired in religion.) Christianity, alone of all "religions," gives birth to a plural, democratic world; alone of all "religions," it begets unfettered human agency. The elemental *human dispossession* that characterizes all religion is paradoxically overcome by and through a unique religion: Christianity. This story of "Western Christianity" as a divine parent metamorphosing into its human offspring (modernity), as transcendence embodying itself in worldly life (secularity), as the particular introducing the universal in thought, is remarkable for the way it mimics the sacred Christian narrative in which Jesus incarnates the divine principle, dies, and is reborn to take his place at the right hand of the Father, a narrative whose telos is the redemption of all humankind. Transcendence thus remains in our redeemed world, our secular "European civilization," although now it has a different content as well as a different place. Santiago Zabala, surveying the postmetaphysical trend in Euro-American philosophy, puts it a little differently. Secularization, he writes, is not merely produced by a Christian past but is also a testament to the enduring presence of Christianity in its post-Christian mode (European civilization).[9]

How then, given the present political climate, are we to understand stories that recount the flourishing of a distinctive European civilization, with Christianity as its historical foundation, always in conflict with another called "Islamic"? As part of a political discourse, these stories assert a *European* identity. Their logical implication is that the absence of "democratic traditions" in Islamic civilization explains Muslim resort to the coercive notion of blasphemy and its inability to grasp the supreme importance of freedom. This appears self-evident. But is it?

From a sociological point of view, populations that belong to "European civilization" are highly differentiated by class, nationalism, and religious identity. They have often been riven by internal conflict, in which warring parties have used the same principle of critical public speech to attack one another, and in which alliances have sometimes been made with Muslim princes. There have always been important movements that have sought to censor public communication in the West, to restrain and control democratic tendencies, in the name of freedom or equality or a stable order. The entire history of European countries in the Americas, Asia, and Africa (with its repressions of the indigenous populations they ruled over) has been an integral part of "European civilization." Hannah Arendt famously argued that the racist policies of European imperialism were essential to the development of fascism in Europe. It is not easy, therefore, to understand what exactly is being claimed when "democracy" and "free speech" are said to be intrinsic to "European civilization," and inequality and repression are attributed to "Islamic civilization."

True, "democratic" institutions are now more firmly established within Western states than in Middle Eastern ones,[10] and the legal systems of Muslim-majority countries were not, until they imported Western law, built around the idea of universal legal equality. But instead of regarding the concern with the particular as opposed to the universal as a *lack*, as an absence that leads to the infliction of social indignities, we might examine more closely the forms in which the universal drive to freedom appears in liberal societies. Thus, one form of universalization central to liberal politics and economics is the *substitutability* of individuals: in the arithmetic of electoral politics, each voter counts as one and is the exact equivalent of every other voter—no more, no less, and no different. Each citizen has the same right to take part in the political process, and to be heard politically, as every other. Substitutability is more fundamental to liberal democracy than electoral consent, from which Western governments are said to derive their legitimacy, because consent here is dependent on counting substitutable votes.

Substitutability is more than a principle of electoral politics. It is also a social technique essential to bureaucratic control and to market manipulation, both being ways of normalizing (and therefore constraining) the individual. This is why statistical modes of thinking and representation—the construction of political and economic strategies on the basis of proportions, averages, trends, and so on—are so important to modern capitalist societies. The fact that individuals have equal value and so may be substituted for one another is, however, what helps to undermine the liberal notion of personal dignity, because for the individual to count as a substitutable unit, his or her uniqueness must be discounted. Thus, even when we use Western criteria of democratic virtue, "liberal European civilization" emerges as highly contradictory.

A word on my use of the term "liberal" in this paper: I am aware that liberalism is a complex historical tradition, that Locke is not Constant and Constant is not Mill and Mill is not Rawls, that the history of liberalism in North America is not the same as that in Europe—or, for that matter, in parts of the global South where it can be said to have a substantial purchase. Liberalism isn't located simply in classical texts, and of course it jostles with other traditions in the West. In its early stages, liberal politics was engaged in challenging hegemonic power, it was full of passion. Now, more often than not, it is the ally of global power: cool, rational, and imperturbable. As a discursive space, liberalism provides its advocates with a common political and moral language in which to identify problems and to dispute them. Such ideas as individual autonomy, freedom of (economic, political, social) exchange, limitation of state power, rule of law, national self-determination, and religious toleration belong to that space, not least when their meanings are debated. Its theorists seek to present liberalism as consistent and unified, but it is precisely the contradictions and ambiguities in the language of liberalism that make the public debates among self-styled liberals and with their "illiberal" opponents possible. Liberalism thus provides moderns with a vocabulary that can cover a multitude of sins—and virtues. The word "liberty" itself has been inserted into a variety of conflicting perspectives—as the political assertions of the American government and that of its critics make evident. I call the society in which political and moral arguments using this vocabulary are sited "liberal." The tradition in which these contradictions are embedded alerts us to the fact that the conflict is not usefully seen as one between "liberal" and "illiberal" tendencies in every civilization or country (as several writers have recently proposed). The conflict is intrinsic to liberalism as an evolving discursive tradition, and what is plausibly liberatory in one context is clearly repressive in another.

Democracy and freedom are central to "Western Civilization," and the universal right to free speech is central to democracy. Or is it? How does the idea of cultivating elite sensibilities (quality) implied by "civilization" fit with the idea of mass equality (quantity) implied by "democracy"? This question was raised in nineteenth-century Britain when the extension of the suffrage was debated. It was then, for example, that Mill argued for a system of plural voting that would give greater weight to the educated ("more civilized") classes to balance the working-class majority.[11] But the problem has remained unresolved. Answers at a philosophical level are plentiful, however, according to which some measure of trust, amicability, and self-reliance are made essential to democracy. For this reason Zabala, whom I cited earlier, believes that secularity provides the key:

> It was Dewey's merit to have argued that we achieve full
> political maturity only at the moment when we succeed in
> doing without any metaphysical culture, without the culture of
> belief in non-human powers and forces. Only after the French
> Revolution did human beings learn to rely increasingly on
> their own powers; Dewey called the religion that teaches men
> to rely on themselves a "religion of love" (the complete oppo-
> site of a "religion of fear") because it is virtually impossible to
> distinguish it from the condition of the citizen who participates
> concretely in democracy.[12]

It is worth stressing, however, that the French Revolution did not simply introduce ideas of solidarity, democracy, and freedom into the modern world. Revolutionary armies sought to promote liberty, equality, and fraternity by conquest. The revolution inaugurated the age of modern empires, unleashing modern warfare, nationalism, racism, and genocide around the world. All of this is certainly part of "Christian" Europe's history. Of course it would be absurd to suggest that it is the sum, or the essence, of Western history, but it *is* a part. Is it not therefore also part of its inheritance? The distinguished philosopher Richard Rorty has talked about rehabilitating the idea of "the European *mission civilizatrice*" with reference to its democratic values—its unique attachment to equality and freedom.[13] But he does not explain who will decide what really represents "European values," how they will be applied, and what they will actually achieve in the world of unequal power. As recent commentators have pointed out, democratic republics are as capable of legislating repression at home and depriving the liberty of weaker peoples abroad, whether by military or economic means.

Liberalism and the Shape of Free Speech

The charge of blasphemy is said to be an archaic religious constraint, and free speech a principle essential to modern freedom. But if the West is a civilization with Christianity as its historical foundation, does the concept of blasphemy have any place in it now that the West is secularized? Are there any resemblances between the idea of blasphemy and the prohibitions established by secular law? Do prohibitions and protections relating to speech tell us something about the idea of "the human" defined by them? And how does the idea of the human serve to distinguish between "the religious" and "the secular"?

If blasphemy indicates a limit transgressed, does secular criticism signify liberation? Modern societies *do*, of course, have legal constraints on communication. Thus there are laws of copyright, patent, and trademark, and laws protecting commercial secrets, all of which prohibit in different ways the free circulation of expressions and ideas. Are property rights in a work of art infringed if it is publicly reproduced in a distorted form by someone other than the original author with the aim of commenting on it? And if they *are* infringed, how does the sense of violation differ from claims about blasphemy? My point here is not that there is no difference, but that there are legal conditions that define what may be communicated freely, and how, in liberal democratic societies, and that consequently the flow of public speech has a particular shape by which its "freedom" is determined.

There are laws that prohibit expression in public and that appear at first sight to have nothing to do with property: for example, indecency laws and laws relating to child pornography, whose circulation is prohibited even in cyberspace. The first set of laws (copyright, and so on) you might say has to do with the workings of a market economy and so with property, whereas the second (pornography) is quite different because it deals with ethics. But although it is the laws relating to the latter whose infringement evokes the greatest passion, both sets of constraint are clues to the liberal secular ideal of the human, the proper subject of all freedoms and rights. Both sets of limits articulate different ways in which property and its protection define the person. In a secular society these laws make it possible to demarcate and defend one's self in terms of what one owns, including, above all, one's body. Thus our conceptions of "trespassing" on another's body and of "exploiting" it are matters of central concern to laws regulating sexual propriety. They also relate to slavery, a nonliberal form of property, for modern law holds that one cannot transfer ownership of one's living body to another person or acquire property rights in another's. Freedom is thus regarded as an inalienable form of property, a capacity that all individual persons possess in a state of nature, rooted in the living body. There are, of course, exceptions to this principle of absolute ownership in one's body, some old and some new: for example, suicide—destroying oneself—is not only forbidden but also regarded by most people in liberal countries with horror, even though the person is said to be the sole owner of the body she inhabits and animates. This exception to self-ownership is often explained by secularists in terms of the humanist principle of "the dignity of human life," a principle that is not seen as conflicting with the brutality of war. Warfare is presented, regretfully, as a mode of killing and dying in the name of one's nation or of universal human redemption.

Apart from this old contradiction there is now a considerable area of legal and moral confusion regarding the ownership of donated human organs and human tissue taken as samples for medical research.[14] This confusion adds to the growing sense that the sacred conception of the self-owning human, the foundation of freedoms in modern society, is under threat. All the more reason, it would seem, for affirming his proprietary rights with vehemence.

In theory, the self-owning liberal subject has the ability to choose freely, a freedom that can be publicly demonstrated. The reality is more complicated. Famously, there are two subject positions—one economic and the other political—whose freedom is invested with value in liberal democratic society, both of which are linked to a conception of the freely choosing self and the limits that protect it. Thus, as a citizen the subject has the right to criticize political matters *openly and freely* and to vote for whichever political candidate she wishes—but she is obliged to do so *in strictest secrecy*. There is a paradox in the fact that the individual choice of candidates must be hidden to be free, while critical speech to be free must be exercised in public. This difference actually indicates that while the former takes for granted that the citizen is embedded in particular social relationships, the latter assumes that he is an abstract individual with universal rights. As an economic individual, the subject is free to work at, spend, and purchase whatever she chooses, and has the right to protect her property legally. Marx was surely right when he pointed out that in modern liberal societies the freedom of the producer is a precondition for the growth of capital—or, as we might put it today, unrestricted consumption is a source of corporate power. What he failed to point out, however, is that *that* power in turn may limit the liberty of the citizen. Social constraint (and, as Freud has made us aware, even psychological constraint) lies at the heart of individual choice. It seems probable, therefore, that the intolerable character of blasphemy accusations in this kind of society derives not so much from their attempt to constrain as from the theological language in which the constraint is articulated. Theology invokes dependence on a transcendental power, and secularism has rejected such a power by affirming human independence. (But let's note that freedom from transcendence is secularism's *formal claim*. In fact, constraint and dependence are massively present in our secular world, transcending the individual subject-agent's ability to know and to act.)

My concern is not to make the banal argument that free speech is never totally free because in a liberal society freedom is balanced by responsibility. Instead I want to ask what the particular patterns of liberal restriction can tell us about liberal ideas of the *free* human. The self-owning individual is a famous liberal idea, and, within that conception, although there are limits to what one may do to oneself, there is greater latitude in relation to one's material property. The ownership of property doesn't only establish immunity in relation to all those who don't own it. It also secures one's right to do with it what one wishes—so long as no damage is done to the rights of others. The right to choose how to dispose of what one owns is integral to the liberal subject—and the subject's body, affections, and speech are regarded as *personal property* because they constitute the person.

I will return to this point about discourse as property, but first I want to introduce a concept central to Islamic traditional thought about free speech but not to liberal thought (or at least not central in the same way)—*seduction*.

In liberal society, rape, the subjection of a person's body against his/her wish for the purpose of sexual enjoyment is a serious crime, whereas seduction—the mere manipulation of another person's desire—is not. The first is a violence; the other is not. In the latter case, no property right is violated. Compare this understanding with that in ancient Greece, where seduction was a more serious crime than rape because it involved the capture of someone's affection and loyalty away from the man to whom they properly belonged.[15] What this indicates is not only that the woman's viewpoint did not matter legally in the ancient world, but also that in liberal society seduction is not considered a violation—except where minors are concerned. In liberal society seduction is not merely permitted, it is positively valued as a sign of individual freedom. Every adult may dispose of his or her body, affections, and speech at will, so long as no harm is done to the property of others. That is why the prohibition of seduction between adults—that is to say, of the public exchange of sexual signals—is regarded as a constraint on natural liberty itself. Such a prohibition is normally regarded as of a piece with the curtailment of free speech.

So how clear is the liberal distinction between coercion and reasoned choice that underlies the notion of free speech? There is, in fact, a large area between these two opposites in which everyday life is lived. The game of seduction—in which both consent and coercion are ambiguously present—is played in this area. And it is in this area, too, that our everyday understanding of liberty is practiced.

Thus in liberal democracies the individual as consumer and as voter is subjected to a variety of allurements through appeals to greed, vanity, envy, revenge, and so on. What in other circumstances may be identified and condemned as moral failings are here essential to the functioning of a particular kind of economy and polity. Numerous studies have described how television as a medium of communication seeks to shape viewers' choices of commodities and candidates. (Film in general works on seducing the audience, even where no political or commercial message is intended.) To seduce is to incite someone to open up his or her innermost self to images, sounds, and words offered by the seducer and to lead the seduced—complicitly or unwittingly—to an end first conceived by the former.

Let me take up again the question of copyright that apparently marks out some of the limits to freedom of speech in liberal society. In a detailed account of the legal disputes over the perpetuity of copyright in late eighteenth-century England, Mark Rose has demonstrated how the idea of incorporeal property (the literary work) emerged through the concept of the author as proprietor. To begin with, those who argued for perpetual copyright did so on the understanding that the author had a natural property right to something he had created. When opponents of unlimited copyright insisted that ideas as such couldn't be considered property, and that copyright should therefore be treated as a limited personal right exactly like a patent, they were countered by the argument that the property being claimed was neither the physical book that could be purchased, nor the ideas communicated, but something made up of style and sentiment. "What we here observe," Rose writes, "is a twin birth, the simultaneous emergence in the discourse of the law of the proprietary author and the literary work. The two concepts are bound to each other."[16]

It should be clear that the law of copyright is not simply a constraint on free communication but also a way of defining how, when, and for whom literary communication (one of the most valued forms of freedom in modern liberal society) can be regarded as free, creative, and inalienable. A person's freedom to say whatever he or she wants, how he or she wants, depends in part on a particular notion of property. It implies a particular kind of property-owning subject whose freedom of speech rests on the truth of what is spoken—that is, created and offered to the public, *but never in its essence alienated*.

Thus, while cultural historians have already written at length on the Romantic vocabulary of national freedom movements, historians of literature have now begun to trace the Romantic roots of the concept of "the literary work" through the mutual shaping of freedom and constraint.[17] It remains to be investigated to what extent the general idea of "freedom of speech" also has those roots. Such a genealogy has still to be mapped so that we can regard it not as the demand of secular reason but as the outcome of a Romantic project aiming at the construction of virtuous human subjects.

What Does the West Understand Blasphemy to Be?

The willful destruction of signs—that is to say, the assault on images and words that are invested with the power to determine what counts as truth—has a long history of transcending the distinction between the religious and the secular. Like iconoclasm and blasphemy, secular critique also seeks to create spaces for new truth, and, like them, it does so by destroying spaces that were occupied by other signs.

The French historian Alain Cabantous once noted that when Jesus claimed for himself a divine nature, his claim was condemned as blasphemy. That blasphemy led to his death, and the death was followed by resurrection. "In this one respect," Cabantous writes, "blasphemy *founded* Christianity."[18] We might add here that every new tradition, whether it is called religious or not, is founded in a discursive rupture—which means through a kind of violence. Cabantous doesn't say this but others have done so. Some have even made the argument that the disruption of blasphemy may be seen as the attempt by a lesser violence to overcome a greater.[19] This may sometimes be the case, but I will only say that it does not follow that every blasphemous utterance is therefore a new founding; blasphemy as an act of violence (whether by the weak or the powerful) may be little more than an *obsession*, in which the act serves as the re-instantiation of an established genre, the restoration of a style *that itself has no foundation and no content*. In other words, blasphemy may simply be violence masquerading as creative rupture.

Cabantous could have observed that in the foundation of Christianity the blasphemy was not perceived as such by *believers*. From a Christian point of view, the *charge* of blasphemy was merely an expression of disbelief. And although that disbelief eventually led to Christ's death, Christians have historically held that the violence done to him was part of a divine plan. Did Christ *know* his unbelieving listeners would take what he said as blasphemy because his crucifixion was essential to the project of human redemption? He was, after all, both man and God. Strictly speaking, of course, what founded Christianity was not blasphemy itself but a new narrative of sacrifice and redemption—a story of martyrdom (witnessing) that would be, for believers, the door to eternal life.

The Truth, said Jesus to his followers, will set you free. The unredeemed human condition is lack of freedom; free speech—truthful speech—releases the human subject from his or her servitude. The truth must be spoken openly even if those who do not possess it regard speaking it freely as blasphemy. In this context a modern New Testament scholar writes: "In spite of the opposition of those who are unbelievers, of those who criticize the apostle [John], the Christian may speak freely because he knows Him who conquers all opposition, because he knows that wonderful communion with God which transcends everything in the world."[20] Of course the liberal principle of free speech does not depend on the proviso that speech to be free must be literally true, but the Christian idea of Truth as applied to speaking and listening freely helps, I think, to explain why that principle has come to be thought of as "sacred."

Blasphemy—a sinful act that is liable to worldly punishment—has a long history in Christianity. In England it became a crime in common law only in the seventeenth century, at a time when national courts were taking over from ecclesiastical courts and the modern state was taking shape. Common law did not distinguish between heresy (the holding of views contrary to church doctrine) and blasphemy (the utterance of insults against God or His saints), as medieval canon law had done. So, from the seventeenth century on, the crime of blasphemy was entangled with the question of political toleration and the formation of the secular modern state. Over the next two centuries, differences of legal opinion arose as to whether public statements lacking defamatory intent or expressed in moderate language were liable to criminal prosecution. It was felt that scholarly debate and discussion needed protection, even if they appeared to be "irreligious." This led to increasing legal attention being paid to the language (that is, style and context) in which "blasphemy" appeared, regardless of how disruptive of established truth it was.

The tendency to emphasize manner of expression—to see blasphemy in terms of form rather than content—had, however, some interesting legal implications: vulgar working-class speech was less protected than the polite speech of the middle and upper classes. A scholar who has studied blasphemy trials in nineteenth-century England calls them "class crimes of language" on account of the class bias they indicate.[21] That an exceptionally large number of them took place during the period when a national state and a class system began to appear is itself of some significance. For this reason I am inclined to say that, rather than simply indicating class bias, the identification of blasphemy helped to constitute class difference in which asymmetrical power was repeatedly inscribed. Therefore I want to suggest that we see blasphemy in these cases not as a discursive device for suppressing free speech but as an indicator of the shape that free speech takes at different times and in different places, reflecting, as it does so, different structures of power and subjectivity.

How Do Muslims Think of the Limits to Free Speech?

What *are* Islamic ideas of blasphemy? Obviously not all Muslims think alike, but questions about Islamic ideas of blasphemy are aimed at a moral tradition. But even that tradition contains divergences, tensions, and instabilities that cannot be attributed to an entire "civilizational people." Nevertheless, I will draw on aspects of that tradition in order to explore further some liberal ideas about freedom. One of these is the assumption that the Islamic tradition is rooted in a more restrictive system of ethics, that it does not allow the freedom (especially the freedom of speech) provided and defended by liberal society. Although there is something to this, the simple notion of liberty that is either present or absent seems to me unsatisfactory here.

It is true that Islamic religious regulation restricts the individual's right to behave as he or she wishes through public prohibition, so that the line between *morality* and *manners* (a crucial distinction for the worldly critic) is obscured and the space of choice narrowed. The worldly critic wants to see and hear everything: nothing is taboo, everything is subject to critical engagement. If speech and behavior are to be constrained, it is because they should conform (willingly?) to civility. Good manners take the place of piety; the private and the public are clearly separated. But the situation on the ground is more complicated than the simple binary (the presence or absence of choice) allows. Consider the following socio-legal situation.

The law in a liberal democracy guarantees the citizen's right to privacy, on which her moral and civic freedom rests. But with the emergence of the welfare state, new tensions arise between the abstract ideal of equality under the law and the particular ways in which the law is applied. The idea that morality is properly a "private" matter and that what is private should not be law's business has, paradoxically, contributed to the passing of legislation intended to deal with "private" trouble cases that force themselves into the legal arena. The legislation has given judges and welfare administrators greater discretion in matters relating to the family (custody, childcare, divorce, alimony, matrimonial property, and inheritance). The sentiment guiding this move is that a more humane way of dealing with conflicts is called for, in which different personal beliefs, emotions, and circumstances can be taken into account. The individuality of the person must be respected, which means it must be fully identified. So discretion and private hearings are necessary. Displays of sensibility and hysteria (inscriptions of emotion on the body) must be observed and assessed. Justice, consequently, becomes individualized. Thus the intervention by social workers into ("private") family life in cases of suspected incest or child neglect or spousal abuse is a function of "public" law authorizing bureaucratic action in "private" domains. In short, although religious morality (piety) is not allowed to impose norms of proper speech and behavior on the individual (as would be the case in Muslim ethics), these legal developments redraw the boundaries of individual freedom. The subject's right to relate to her own children is circumscribed by the welfare agency's right to inspect and intervene in that relationship. New sensibilities regarding what is decent—and therefore also what is outrageous—are created, especially in the domain of sexual relations. The uninvited intrusion into domestic space, the breaching of "private" domains, is disallowed in Islamic law, although conformity in "public" behavior may be much stricter. Thus, the limits of freedom are differently articulated in relation to spaces that may roughly be described as "private" and "public," and different kinds of discourse are socially available to distance what is repugnant, whether transcendent or worldly.

This brings me to the Islamic vocabulary that overlaps in some respects with *blasphemy*, a category that defines an outrageous "religious" transgression in the Christian tradition.

Although the Arabic word *tajdīf* is usually glossed in English as "blasphemy" and is used by Christian Arabs to identify what in European religious history is called "blasphemy," Arabic speakers, in the case of the Danish cartoons, did not (so far as I am aware) employ it. The theological term *tajdīf* has the particular sense of "scoffing at God's bounty."[22] Of course, there are other words that overlap with the English word *blasphemy* (for example, *kufr*, "apostasy, blasphemy, infidelity"; *ridda*, "apostasy"; *fisq*, "moral depravity"; and *ilhād*, "heresy, apostasy"), but these were not, to my knowledge, used in response to the Danish cartoons. As accusations against non-Muslim journalists, they would, in any case, be inappropriate. When the World Union of Muslim Scholars made its statement on the Danish cartoons affair, for example, it used the word *isā'ah*, not *tajdīf*. And *isā'ah* has a range of meanings, including "insult, harm, and offense," that are applied in secular contexts.[23] (One of the cartoons, it will be recalled, depicts the Prophet Muhammad as a suicide bomber—a figure at once absurd and barbaric.) The World Union states that it has purposely let a long time pass in order to allow the efforts of numerous Islamic and Arab organizations, and several states, to elicit an appropriate expression of remorse, but the wait has been to no avail. Therefore "the Union will be obliged to call upon the millions of Muslims in the world to boycott Danish and Norwegian products and activities."[24] The freedom to campaign against particular consumer goods is opposed to the freedom to criticize beliefs publicly: One social weapon faced another, each employing a different aspect of the modern idea of freedom. If physical violence was sometimes used by some of those who advocated a boycott, this should not obscure the fact that a commercial boycott is always a kind of violence, especially if it is infused with anger, because it attacks people's livelihood. The European history of boycotts (the refusal to purchase commodities) and strikes (the withholding of labor), with all their accompanying violence, has been a story of the struggle for modern rights. And yet in the present case European commentators described the two differently: the one as an expression of freedom, the other as an attempt at restricting it, and thus as yet another sign of the conflict between two civilizations having opposed political orientations. In liberal democratic thinking the principle of free speech cannot be curtailed by the offense its exercise may cause—so long as it is not defamatory or a threat to social order.

More interesting than the political defense of free speech was the philosophical argument that it was even a good thing that pious Muslims felt injured, because being hurt by criticism might provoke people to reexamine their beliefs—something vital both for democratic debate and for ethical decision making. This point, in contrast to the first, valorizes the consequence of free speech rather than the act itself. The criticism of questionable (religious) beliefs is presented as an obligation of free speech, an act carried out in the belief that truth is power. Many even in post-Christian Western society agree with the Christian claim that *the truth makes one free* (John 8:32).

That this is not an Islamic formulation emerges from an examination of the widely discussed trial of Nasr Hamid Abu Zayd, a professor at Cairo University, for apostasy (*ridda*) because he had advocated a radically new interpretation of the revealed text of the Qur'an.[25] Of course both *truth* and *freedom* are greatly valued in the Islamic tradition, but they are not tied up together quite as they are in Christianity. (It may be pointed out in passing that the many cases of apostasy in the contemporary Middle East that have received so much publicity in the West are actually relatively recent and closely connected with the formation of the modern nation-state, a modern judiciary, and the rise of modern politics. In this context one may recall the burst of blasphemy trials in nineteenth-century England to which I referred earlier.) A question worth considering, however, is whether these trials should be seen solely in terms of the suppression of freedom: What do they tell us about the liberal idea of the human subject?

In a book that deals with the Abu Zayd case,[26] Islamist lawyer Muhammad Salīm al-'Awwa emphasizes that the Sharia (the "religious law") guarantees freedom of belief. "Freedom of belief means the right of every human being to embrace whatever ideas and doctrines he wishes, even if they conflict with those of the group in which he lives or to which he belongs, or conflicts with what the majority of its members regard as true."[27] He goes on to say that no one may exert pressure to get another to reveal his/her religious beliefs—that is to say, the Sharia prohibits the use of inquisitorial methods.[28] The right to think whatever one wishes does not, however, include the right to express one's religious or moral beliefs publicly with the intention of converting people to a false commitment. Such a limitation may seem strange to modern liberals (although it was not strange to Kant),[29] for whom the ability to speak publicly about one's beliefs is necessary to freedom. It is, after all, one aspect of "the freedom of religion" that is guaranteed by a secular liberal democracy. Al-'Awwa is aware of this, and he cites two Qur'anic verses that seem to guarantee freedom of religion: *lā ikrāha fi-ddīn*, "There is no compulsion in religion" (2:256), and *faman shā'a falyu'min wa man shā'a falyakfur*, "let him who wills have faith, and him who wills reject it" (18:29). But for the community, what matters is the Muslim subject's social practices—including verbal publication—not her internal thoughts, whatever these might be. In contrast, the Christian tradition allows that thoughts can commit the sin of blasphemy and should therefore be subject to discipline: thoughts are subject to confession.[30]

According to al-'Awwa, publishing one's thoughts changes their character, makes them publicly accessible signs: "To publish something," he quotes an old saying, "is to lay oneself open to the public."[31] It is one thing to think whatever one wishes, he argues, and a different thing to seduce others into accepting commitments that are contrary to the moral order. In a well-known book published in Lebanon in 1970, responding to the accusation of apostasy against the Syrian philosopher Jalal Sadiq al-'Azm for his famous *Naqd al-fikr al-dīnī* (*The Critique of Religious Thought*; 1969), Shaykh 'Uthman Safi makes a similar distinction but without reference to Islamic religious authorities. His approach instead is to make an explicit distinction between "natural, innate freedom" and freedom as defined and limited by the law. The individual may give free rein to his thought and imagination, accepting or rejecting as he wishes within the limits of what he contemplates. "When these possibilities of freedom that the human being enjoys remain within his soul, the law, especially, cannot interfere with them except when the belief is moved from secrecy to broad daylight [*min as-sirr ila al-jahr*]."[32] When, in the Abu Zayd case, the highest court of appeal in Egypt distinguished between the inviolability enjoyed by private belief and the vulnerability of published statements to the charge of *kufr* ("apostasy, blasphemy, infidelity"), the court was saying that the legal *meaning* of the latter was not to be decided by its *origin* in the intention of a particular author but by its *function* in a social relation. The effect of his making them public was therefore his responsibility. This position is close to, but not identical with, a modern liberal view.

The liberal view, in general, assumes that the crucial relationship in this matter is between two things: a person, on the one hand, and the written or spoken words he or she asserts and believes to be true (assents mentally to) on the other. These statements are—like all empirical statements—subject to criteria of verification. Belief, however, has an ambiguous status—at once internal and external. It is the internal sense that most modern Westerners have taken as being primary, although it is generally recognized that it is possible to externalize it. Thus, when Kilian Bälz writes that "belief is a spiritual affair which is not readily accessible to investigation in the court room,"[33] he is restating the secular idea of "religious belief" understood as a private spiritual matter. But the statement that "religious belief" is not readily accessible in a courtroom should be understood, I suggest, as a claim of immunity (the court has no right to intrude) rather than of principled skepticism about the court's practical ability to extract the absolute truth. It is quite different, in other words, from the classical Sharia tradition, in which Islamic jurists adopt the principle of epistemological skepticism, insisting that the judge cannot distinguish with absolute certainty a truthful utterance from a lie when that is unsupported by sensory experience. Although divine revelation, together with the tradition of the Prophet and the consensus of jurists, *do* provide Muslims with "indisputable and certain knowledge" (*'ilm yaqin*), jurists held that this certainty relates to the legal and ethical rules they establish and not to the truth of what claimants say are facts in a given case.[34] A secular state, by contrast, has to determine whether a particular doctrine or practice belongs to a "religion"—a particular "religion"—and therefore qualifies the believer or practitioner to equal treatment with members of other "religions."[35] Hence belief *must* be externalizable as doctrine ("I hold the following things to be true"), whether voluntarily or by force.

The issue in the Abu Zayd case is not the correctness or otherwise of "belief" in this sense, but the legal and social consequences of a Muslim professor's teaching a doctrine that was said to be contrary to Islamic commitment.[36] (The Arabic word *imān* is often translated into English as "belief"—as in the frequently used Qur'anic phrase *ayyuhal-mu'minīn*, "O Believers!"—but is better rendered as "faith," as in "I shall be faithful to you." Another word commonly glossed as "belief," *i'tiqād*, derives from the root *'aqada*, "to put together." This root gives the word *'aqd*, "contract," and its many cognates, and thus carries a sense of social relationship. Its primary sense in classical Arabic is the bond that commits the believer to God.)[37] In the classic Sharia position, the strength of personal conviction is said to be a matter between the individual and his God (*baynahu wa bayna rabbih*). Belief in this context is understood as a continuum rather than as a binary (belief/disbelief or certainty/doubt) so that it is possible to describe someone as "weakly believing."

Disbelief incurs no legal punishment; even the Qur'an stipulates no worldly punishment for disbelief. In the classical law, punishment for apostasy is justified on the grounds of its political and social consequences, not of entertaining false doctrine itself. Put another way, insofar as the law concerns itself with disbelief, it is not as a matter of its propositional untruth but of a solemn social relationship being openly repudiated ("being unfaithful"). Legally, apostasy (*ridda, kufr*) can therefore be established only on the basis of the functioning of external signs (including public speech or writing, publicly visible behavior), never on the basis of inferred or forcibly extracted internal belief.[38]

In contemporary Egypt, conviction of a Muslim for apostasy in a court of law has consequences for civil status because the Sharia is the law of personal status there. One consequence is the automatic dissolution of an apostate's marriage if it was contracted according to the Sharia. There are also social consequences, among them the concern that an apostate who is responsible for teaching Islamic thought may suppress the truth through the unrestrained publications of spoken and written signs. (This point should not be confused with the judgment of the Court of Appeal in the Abu Zayd case when it declared that an attack on Islam is an attack on the foundations of Egypt as a Muslim state. *That* consequentialist argument—as well as claims that the feelings of Muslims are offended—is quite different.)

The crucial distinction made in liberal thought between *seduction* and *forcible subjection* to which I referred earlier, in which the former is legally permitted and the latter penalized, is here absent—at least in al-'Awwa's argument. To seduce someone is to connive at rendering him or her unfaithful, to make the other break an existing social commitment. Even in medieval Christendom, the term *infidelitas* could be used not only in relation to personal departures from authorized doctrine but also, in a secular sense, to breaking a contract.[39] "Unfaithfulness" in this worldly sense now has a quaint ring about it in modern liberal society and relates only to sexual seduction.

In Islamic theology, seduction is a matter of great concern—and not merely in the sexual sense. The Qur'an contains numerous words that can be glossed as "seducing" and "deluding"—among them the verbal roots *fatana, rāwada, gharra. Fatana* (from which comes the familiar noun *fitna*) always has the sense of "temptation and affliction as a testing," of "persecution, treachery, or social strife."[40] But the temptation referred to by this term in the Qur'an is not sexual. (Even in modern Arabic, *fitna* is not used exclusively in a sexual sense; it can also mean enchantment and fascination generally.) It is the word *rāwada* that is used in the Qur'an to refer explicitly to sexual seduction. *Gharra* refers to delusion through attachment to fancies, to the act of deceiving oneself. The nominal form *ighrā'* can be glossed as "excessive attachment, self-love, desire, incitement," but it also connotes social unrest and instability. Muslim theologians and jurists assumed that seduction in all its forms was necessarily dangerous not only for the individual (because it indicated a loss of self-control) but for the social order too (it could lead to violence and civil discord). They were wrong, of course, because they didn't know about market democracy, a system that thrives on the consumer's loss of self-control and one in which politicians have learned to seduce their audiences while maintaining overall political stability.

So under what circumstances can one say that one is choosing what one truly believes—or that one's true beliefs are expressed only when one chooses freely? On the other hand, when can one say that it is in expressing one's beliefs *because one must* that one provides evidence of what one's true beliefs are?

According to Susan Mendus,[41] John Locke propounded his theory of political toleration on the basis of the psychological principle that belief can never be determined by the will. This principle rests on a new psychology of the will that was beginning to emerge in seventeenth-century Europe, as well as a new understanding of "belief." In the Middle Ages a contrary doctrine prevailed. Thomas Aquinas, for example, took it for granted that belief (a commitment, a holding dear) could indeed be willed. It was this modern psychology that allowed Locke to insist that the Prince's attempt to coerce religious belief—including belief in the salvational implications of religious practices—was irrational. All that force could secure was an insincere profession of faith. Of course, the Prince might have other reasons for imposing conformity on his subjects than their salvation—such as upholding law and order—that would not render his coercive efforts necessarily irrational. The presumption that political attempts to coerce belief are irrational because they are impossible has been the focus of much debate summarized by Mendus. The Muslim position, as expounded by al-'Awwa, is different from Locke's. Since, according to the latter, it is impossible to coerce belief, the mind becomes the site of true religious belonging, and physical force as the arm of civil government should therefore confine itself to civil interests—the protection of life, limb, and property—only. According to the former, religious *belonging*, as distinct from religious belief, *can* be forced, or seduced, but it is illegitimate to do so. (This accords, incidentally, with the central Islamic tradition about Christians and Jews, whose understanding of divine revelation is considered to be distorted—the Qur'an is perfect—*but who are not therefore required to abjure their error.*) What matters, finally, is belonging to a particular way of life in which the person does not own himself.

Mendus's view is that Locke was right to make the presumption about the impossibility of coercing religious belief, and she defends him against his critics on this point by making what she regards a critical distinction within the individual's consciousness—a difference between *sincere* and *authentic* belief—that she borrows from Bernard Williams. This allows her to argue that a forcible conversion (brainwashing) may at most obtain a *sincere* belief, not an *authentic* one. But the conditions cited by Mendus—beginning with the so-called acceptance condition—are, I think, questionable. Thus her claim that the alternatives of deliberate reticence (not saying what one really believes) and insincerity (affirming what one doesn't believe) must *always* exist as possibilities in order to determine whether a belief is really authentic or genuine seems to me unconvincing. The alternatives at issue must surely signify something more than abstract *possibilities*; they must be to the person concerned *real options*, within a given socio-psychological situation, from among which he can actually choose. But if that is so, then certain kinds of religious acts are ruled out a priori: "bearing witness" in public where one feels *one has no choice* but to speak the truth—in anger, say, or in compassion—would have to be identified as "inauthentic."[42] Should the impossibility of remaining silent about what one believes to be morally right in such situations—or the impossibility of saying what one does *not* believe—be taken to mean that the belief is inauthentic?

It is hard to avoid the conclusion that this talk of philosophical criteria determining "authentic belief" is little more than a way of devaluing moral passion, of disregarding the way passion constitutes moral actions so as to render the language of choice irrelevant. One consequence of that devaluation is that it becomes difficult for the secular liberal to understand the passion that informs those for whom, rightly or wrongly, *it is impossible to remain silent when confronted with blasphemy*, those for whom blasphemy is neither "freedom of speech" nor the challenge of a new truth but something that seeks to disrupt a living relationship.

It is important to note that passionate reaction to "blasphemers" is typically directed not at the latter's disbelief but at their alleged violence. I stress that I make no claim to know the real motives of all those who protest against blasphemy. My argument is that we will not understand "blasphemy" if all we see in it is a threat to freedom—even though it is true that, historically, powerful punitive apparatuses have usually accompanied the charge of "blasphemy."

Historical Notes on the Idea of Secular Criticism

In an essay entitled "Secular Criticism," the noted literary critic Edward Said wrote that "[c]riticism...is always situated, it is skeptical, secular, reflectively open to its own failings."[43] To this I would merely add three questions: First, what work does the notion "secular" do here? Does it refer to an authority or a sensibility? Second, since criticism employs judgment, since it seeks conviction—of oneself and others—to what extent does it therefore seek to overcome skepticism? Finally, if secular criticism regards itself as confronting the powerful forces of repression, finds itself open to all "failings," can we say that secular criticism aspires to be *heroic*?

So: *what is critique?*

This, of course, is the title of a well-known late essay by Michel Foucault, which began as a lecture originally given at the Sorbonne on 27 May 1978.[44] In the essay Foucault seeks to equate critique with the Kantian notion of Enlightenment and thus to present critique as the singular characteristic of the modern West: "[It] seems that between the lofty Kantian enterprise and the small polemico-professional activities that bear the name 'critique,' there was in the modern West (dating, roughly, from the fifteenth to the sixteenth century) a certain manner of thinking, of speaking, likewise of acting, and a certain relation to what exists, to what one knows, to what one does, as well as a relation to society, to culture, to others, and all this one might name 'the critical attitude'" (p. 382). It is not clear whether Foucault wishes us to understand that "the critical attitude" is a characteristic only of the modern West, or that "the critical attitude" distinctive of the modern West is quite different from what is found elsewhere—an attitude that enables it to think for the first time of "the transcendent" in a way that permits humanity to make its own future. At any rate, it is clear that in Foucault's view to be enlightened is to adopt a critical attitude, and to engage in critique, as the West has done for several centuries, is equivalent to living in Enlightenment: living heroically, as Kant put it at the beginning of that venture. This seems to me somewhat surprising coming from a genealogist, because it sets aside the need to think through the various historical determinants whose effect—in different circumstances—has been a diversity of "critiques," a diversity of styles, uses, and objectives. Neither the concept nor the practice of critique has a simple history, and that genealogy has yet to be written. What follows is simply a set of disparate historical notes (in which I do not, incidentally, offer any fixed definition of critique, and therefore do not follow any strict distinction between criticism and critique).

The word *criticism* has its origin in the Greek verb *krino*, meaning "to separate," "to decide," "to judge," "to fight," "to accuse." It seems to have been first used in the juridical sphere, where both the act of accusing and the giving of a verdict were called *krino*, and thus referred to the ability to differentiate, to ask probing questions, and to judge. In this worldly arena the semantic beginnings of what we now call "critique" did not aspire to conquer universal truth but to resolve particular crises justly and to correct particular virtues within a particular way of life.[45]

Criticism could also take the form of "free and open speech [*parrhesia*]" in the political forum. Critical preaching, especially associated with the Cynic philosophers of the fourth century BC, was directed at everyone, and its aim was to teach people how to assess their own personal mode of life.[46] Christianity drew on this tradition of free and open speech, transforming the word *parrhesia* in the process to its own end. Criticism and the open call to Truth have remained an important part of popular preaching throughout the Christian era.

In the late medieval period, friars preached in public places, censuring particular ways of living and advocating the Truth. At an academic level, the idea of critique was employed in a number of university disciplines, but not until the theological disputes of the Reformation did it denote the same notion regardless of whether it was applied to classical texts, the Bible, or social life. So to the question, what is critique? the answer would then more often than not have been: The evaluation and interpretation of the truth of scripture.

At first, criticism aimed only at the production of an authentic text and at its meaning, but eventually, as it began to be concerned with the reality represented in the texts, it became what would be called historical criticism—of the newly recovered Greek texts as well as of the scriptures themselves. Pierre Bayle, the seventeenth-century skeptic, exemplifies this development.[47] For him, critique was the activity that separated reason from revelation by the systematic exposure of errors and by the rhetoric of ridicule. In effect, Bayle tried to analyze and dissolve each theory by a continuous demand for reasons, and so to demonstrate that everything confidently accepted on the grounds of reason could be undone by critical reasoning. The use of critique here turned out to be as much an argument for the necessity of faith as it was an attack on the absolute reliability of reason. This was not the old theological use of reason to underwrite revelation, but a new, secular demonstration that if critique is pushed far enough it collapses under its own weight. Politically, Bayle's extreme skepticism was premised on the notion of an egalitarian "republic of letters," in which one could engage equally with others instead of submitting to authority. In the newly emerging discipline of experimental philosophy, criticism took a prudent middle position between skepticism and credulity. In this seventeenth-century culture of knowledge production, social trust and gentlemanly authority became—as Steven Shapin has shown—the basis of reliable testimony and restrained criticism.[48]

At the end of the eighteenth century, Kantianism dominated philosophical discourse. Of course philosophy was not the only mode in which criticism was publicly conducted. A variety of representational forms, unconnected with philosophy, drew on the rich tradition of literary and rhetorical devices to attack social pretensions and political corruption. But the downgrading of rhetoric in nineteenth-century language theories reinforced the claims of philosophy to a unique conceptual domain within which *rational critique* could be properly defined and practiced.

For Kantians, political revolution thus appeared as the alternative to philosophical criticism; freedom for philosophical critique even became a condition of forestalling political revolution. It was Kant who replaced the model of the "republic of letters" with another model: the "court of reason." This followed not only from his direct philosophical concern with *judgment* but also indirectly from his view that truth was guaranteed not by freedom from political and ecclesiastical constraint but by the progress of rational science. To the "court of reason" was given the important task of imposing peace on the apparently unending war of doctrines. For Enlightenment philosophers prior to Kant, critique had been rooted in a secularized metaphysics (in the idea of human reason) and directed against ecclesiastical and state pretensions. For Kant, critique became the process of epistemological self-correction by strict reference to established rational limits and the fixed boundary between private faith and public reason. But his formula for critique as an inquiry into the preconditions of scientific truths cut it off from politics as well as from faith. In Kant's political philosophy it is *law*, not critique, that ends the chaos of metaphysics and holds the corrosive effects of skepticism in check. And its concern is no longer with mundane life but with epistemology.

Only when the Romantics returned to problems of aesthetics was the dominance of Kantian discourse challenged in philosophy. The most prominent figure here is Hegel, who took critique to be immanent in history: transcendental reason and phenomenal object (thought and reality) should not be separated, as Kant had separated them. They are both, Hegel maintained, dialectical constituents of the real—contradictory parts of a developing self and of a world in the process of becoming. In this way, Hegelians set aside the Kantian discipline of epistemology. From this move emerged the famous Marxian dictum that critical theory—the activity of criticizing publicly—is itself a part of social reality.

Marx's Hegelian premise that the existing world is characterized by contradictions led him, however, to the anti-Hegelian conclusion that their removal depended not on new philosophical interpretations but on the practical transformation of reality itself. The reality to be transformed was politico-economic, not moral. In a rapidly industrializing world, critique and revolutionary violence thus no longer appeared as alternatives but as complementary forms of class struggle, and the critical politics this called for was the politics of organized working-class movements.[49]

In the twentieth century, neo-Kantians again limited the concept of critique to epistemology, with the intention of opposing Hegelianism and Marxism. Critique then became a weapon directed at ideological politics and radical intellectuals. Among this group of philosophers, criticism again became the criterion of universal reason, a principle held to be crucial for the natural *and* the human sciences. They defined a scientific fact as one that can be criticized—and that can therefore be falsified. Because religious values are immune to rational critique, because they are based on *faith*, they are neither neutral nor objective, and they cannot therefore have the authority of scientific facts. To the extent that a "belief" is presented as a candidate for truth, it must be held provisionally—that is to say, it must not be taken too seriously. Falsificationists like Popper reaffirmed a more direct connection between epistemology (what are the criteria for valid knowledge about the world) and politics (how can one legitimately use power to make or remake the social world). Because our scientific knowledge of the world is inevitably limited, so they argued, only piecemeal criticism and reform of the social world was rational.[50]

My final example is of secular critique as modern theology. Theology has never been without criticism, and, especially since the beginning of the nineteenth century, theology has absorbed secular criticism. The example I now cite deals with metacriticism: the Regensburg lecture by Pope Benedict XVI in 2006, whose opening salvo against Islam evoked predictable anger from

Muslims across the world.[51] What he believed he was doing in this lecture is not of concern to me here. What *is* interesting is the way he links his discursive attack on Islam to his critique of European reason. According to Benedict, Islamic theology separates the concept of God from reason (making God utterly unpredictable, therefore irrational), whereas Christianity maintains their inseparability in its harmonization of Hellenic rationality with the status of the divine: "In the beginning was the *logos*, and the *logos* is God, says the Evangelist." According to Benedict, this fusion explains why Christianity seeks to lead the individual to the Truth through reasoned persuasion, and why Islam, in contrast, uses force to convert non-Muslims and to punish people for holding false beliefs. The inner rapprochement between biblical faith and Greek philosophical inquiry that constituted Christianity "was an event of decisive importance not only from the standpoint of the history of religions, but also from that of world history—it is an event that concerns us even today." Hence, Benedict's critique of the successive waves of de-Hellenization in European thought—from the Reformation via Kant and liberal theology to scientific positivism—by which, he claims, the inner bond between faith and reason is ruptured. In spite of his polemic against what he takes to be Islamic doctrine (and therefore, arguably, against Muslim immigrants in Europe) and in spite of his assertion that Europe is fundamentally Christian, Benedict's critique is not merely political: it is aimed, in a very secular way, at reaffirming the identification of reason with divinity. His critique of de-Hellenization deals with what he regards as a dangerous restriction of reason's scope—and he calls, therefore, for an unrestricted pursuit and enunciation of the truth. The truth must be presented publicly even if those not possessing it regard the presentation as outrageous—as blasphemy. This is how Benedict concludes his university lecture: "This attempt… at a critique of modern reason from within has nothing to do with putting the clock back to the time before the Enlightenment and rejecting the insights of the modern age... The scientific ethos, moreover, is—as you yourself mentioned, Magnificent Rector—*the will to be obedient to the truth*, and, as such, it embodies an attitude which belongs to the essential decisions of the Christian spirit." Thus, while for Kant critical reason appeals to transcendental law (while paradoxically insisting on the autonomy of the individual subject), Benedict gestures to a Christian life of obedience that accepts *logos* as at once persuasive *reason* and divine *authority*. The Christian obeys not simply because she thinks it reasonable to do so but also because the authority of the truth *compels her to obey*. This Christian critique thus offers to accommodate the "insights" of the scientific ethos but also claims to found itself in the authority of the church.

The modern philosophers I've mentioned—Kant, Hegel, Popper—were all attached to universities, and it is in universities that critique of one kind or another has become essential to useful knowledge production. *Professional* critique, however, has less to do with the right of free speech than with the reproduction of intellectual disciplines and the culture of belief that goes with them. Jon Roberts and James Turner, in *The Sacred and Secular University*, have described the emergence of the modern university in the United States, together with its secular culture, starting in the last quarter of the nineteenth century. They recount how the marginalization or exclusion of formal "religion" in the American university was accompanied by an emphasis on research, professionalization, and specialization, and how these things, in turn, led to a fragmentation of the traditional map of knowledge, which had until then been articulated in a theological language. It was in this situation that the humanities eventually emerged out of the traditions of moral philosophy and philology, and restored coherence to knowledge while according it a distinctive "religious" aura. One consequence was that a less sectarian, less doctrinal idea of religion became part of a liberal culture and therefore part of its understanding of criticism. "This new edition of liberal education had two key elements," they write. "The first was to acquaint students with beauty, especially as manifest in 'poetry' broadly conceived.... A second element thus entered the humanities: a stress on continuities linking the 'poetry' of one era to that of succeeding periods and ultimately our own." Hence, there developed a sharper sense of imparting the moral essence of European civilization to students in higher education through the study of great literature and the conviction that *literary criticism* was the disciplined means to that end. This is one aspect of criticism that has religious roots without being religious, with its emphasis not on *doubt* but on a particular kind of cultivation of the self. But there is another.

Over the last few centuries, modern powers have encouraged and used the developing sciences to normalize and regulate social life—and therefore have legitimized a particular kind of disciplinary criticism. That is why, perhaps, critique that is integral to the growth of useful knowledge—and therefore of modern power—is part of a process whose major lineaments have not been effectively reduced to skepticism, a process that is rarely itself the object of effective public critique. Thus, while the freedom to criticize is represented as being at once a right and a duty of the modern individual, its truth-producing capacity remains subject to disciplinary criteria, while its material conditions of existence (laboratories, buildings, research funds, publishing houses, personal computers, etc.) are provided and watched over by corporate and state power to ensure that citizens can be *useful*.

IN PRESENTING THESE NOTES on thoughts about critique, I have tried to underline the very different understandings people have had of it in Western history, understandings that can't be reduced to the simple distinction between secular criticism (freedom and reason) and religious criticism (intolerance and obscurantism). The practice of secular criticism is now a sign of the modern, of the modern subject's relentless pursuit of truth and freedom, of his or her political agency. It has almost become a *duty*, closely connected to the right to free expression and communication.

But every critical discourse has institutional conditions that define what it is, what it recognizes, what it aims at, what it is destroying—and why. Neither philosophical nor literary criticism can successfully claim to be the privileged site of reason. It matters whether the criticism/critique in question is conducted in the form of parody and satire, confession of sins, political autocritique, professional criticism, or speech under analysis. One might say that if these are all possible instances of critique/criticism, then what we have here is a family concept for which it is not possible to provide a single theory because the *practices* that constitute them differ radically.

And yet there is, perhaps, something distinctive after all about the historical concept of "critique" that Foucault wanted to identify, something other than the varieties of critical practice to which I have pointed: In some areas of our modern life, there is the insistent demand that reasons be given for almost everything. The relation to knowledge, to action, and to other persons *that results when this demand is taken as the foundation of all understanding* is perhaps what Foucault had in mind when he spoke of critique.

"The critical attitude" is the essence of secular heroism.

Blasphemy as the Breaking of Taboo

The recent European discourse on blasphemy as applied to the behavior of Muslim immigrants in Europe serves, paradoxically, at once to confirm and to deny difference. Angry Muslim responses to the publication of the Danish cartoons are seen by secularists as attempting to reintroduce a category that was once a means of oppression in Europe, while they see themselves critiquing, in the name of freedom, the power to suppress human freedom. For the worldly critic, there can be no acceptable taboos. When limits are critiqued, taboos disappear and freedom is expanded. This criticism doesn't merely liberate ideas from taboos, however; it also reinforces the existing distinction between the paradigmatically human and candidates for inclusion in true humanity who do not as yet own their bodies, emotions, and thoughts. It reinforces, in other words, the ideological status of European Muslims as not fully human because they are not yet morally autonomous and politically disciplined.

The modern problem of blasphemy, one might say, is a European invention. For a secular society that doesn't acknowledge the existence of such a thing as blasphemy, it is quite remarkable how much public discourse there is about it—and about those who complain of it or claim to be affronted by it. Quite remarkable, too, is the obsessive need to repeat again and again the words and images that secularists know will be regarded by the pious with horror. Who, one might wonder, are these defenders of worldly criticism trying to convince? It is too simple, I think, to claim—as some Danish commentators have done—that the publication of the cartoons merely sought to overcome the crippling fear that Europeans had of criticizing Muslims.[52] But there is certainly something complicated going on beyond the rational defense of political freedom, something that may have to do with reassuring the limitless self by making a distinction between good and bad violence, with a desire that is impossible.

The limits to possible forms of action are articulated by social values. And of course all such limits are invested with potential violence, even (especially) the value of limitless self-creation. Certainly the violent language and the riots that greeted the Danish cartoons are evidence of one kind of concern about limits. But so too are the modern wars (preemptive and humanitarian) that seek to establish a particular moral order in the world or to make liberal democracy safe within its own bounded spaces—in "Fortress Europe."

Here is a final thought: What would happen if religious language were to be taken more seriously in secular Europe and the preventable deaths in the global South of millions from hunger and war was to be denounced as "blasphemy," as the flouting of ethical limits for the sake of what is claimed to be freedom? What if this were to be done without any declarations of "belief," and yet done in all seriousness as a way of rejecting passionately the aspiration to totalized global control? Of course Europe's proscription of theological language in the political domain makes such a use of the word "blasphemy" inconceivable. But does this impossibility merely signal a secular reluctance to politicize "religion," or is it the symptom of an incapacity?

This question is not intended as a moral reproof but as an invitation to look again at an empirical feature of modernity, especially the notion of secular criticism.

An earlier version of this essay was published as "Reflections on Blasphemy and Secular Criticism," in Hent de Vries, ed., Religion: Beyond a Concept *(New York, 2007).*

Endnotes

[1] On September 30, 2005, the Danish newspaper *Jyllands-Posten* published a number of cartoons of the Prophet Muhammad, an act seen as insulting to him by many Muslims. The result was widespread protest and controversy in Europe and elsewhere.

[2] The Western press has made much of the irrational violence of Muslims responding to the publication of the cartoons, but it has rarely noted the political atmosphere in which Muslims live in Europe generally and in Denmark particularly. According to a Danish researcher, respectable members of parliament from a variety of Danish parties made the following statements to the national press in the 2001 elections: "Muslims are just waiting for the right moment to kill us" (Mogens Camre, Progress Party); "Certain people pose a security risk solely because of their religion, which means that they have to be placed in internment camps" (Inge Dahl Sorensen, Liberal Party); "If you try to legislate your way out of these problems [concerning Muslim organizations], it is a historical rule that rats always find new holes if you cover up the old ones" (Poul Nyrup Rasmussen, Social Democratic Party). Quoted in P. Hervik, "The Emergence of Neo-Nationalism in Denmark, 1992–2001," in *Neo-Nationalism in Europe and Beyond: Perspectives from Social Anthropology,* ed. Marcus Banks and Andre Gingrich (Oxford, 2006).

[3] "The prolonged and violent demonstrations against the Danish cartoons," wrote George Packer, *New Yorker* staff writer, "were a staged attempt by Islamists to intimidate their enemies in their own countries and in the West"; "Fighting Faiths: Can liberal internationalism be saved?" *New Yorker,* July 10 and 17, 2006, pp. 95–96.

[4] "For example, parts of the Danish press as well as Danish politicians have recently argued that Islamic Studies scholars are acting as political agents because they intentionally choose to disregard certain topics, such as social processes in which Islam can be seen as an obstacle to integration and/or a potential security threat"; from *Research on Islam Repositioned,* theme statement for seminar sponsored by Danish research network *Forum for the Research on Islam* (FIFO), University of Copenhagen, May 14–15, 2007. And yet, according to the first Europol report on terrorism published in 2007, it appears that of 498 acts of terrorism that took place in the European Union during 2006, Islamists were responsible for only one. The largest number was carried out by Basque separatists, and only one of these Basque attacks resulted in loss of life. Yet more than half

of those arrested on suspicion of terrorism were Muslim. Almost all the media in Europe have ignored these figures while playing up "the threat of Islam." What, one wonders, accounts for this curious voluble silence?

5   Lecture of the Holy Father, "Faith, Reason, and the University: Memories and Reflections," September 2006, University of Regensberg, Germany: http://www.vatican.va/holy_father/benedict_xvi/speeches/2006/september/documents/hf_ben-xvi_spe_20060912_university-regensburg_en.html. In contrast, the distinguished Catholic philosopher Charles Taylor speaks of "the unbridgeable gulf between Christianity and Greek philosophy." See the introduction to his *The Secular Age* (Cambridge, MA, 2007).

6   Francis Fukuyama, *The End of History and the Last Man,* afterword to the reprint edition (New York, 2006). See also the dialogue between an American nonreligious postmodern philosopher and an Italian Christian postmodern theologian, in which both agree on the fundamental link between Christianity and democracy: Richard Rorty and Gianni Vattimo, *The Future of Religion,* ed. Santiago Zabala (New York, 2005).

7   George Grote, *History of Greece* (London, 2001).

8   Marcel Gauchet, *The Disenchantment of the World: A Political History of Religion,* foreword by Charles Taylor (Princeton, 1997).

9   See Santiago Zabala's essay "A Religion Without Theists or Atheists," which introduces Rorty and Vattimo, *Future of Religion,* p. 2.

10   The Middle East is not, of course, equivalent to "the world of Islam"—or even to "Muslim-majority countries," since most Muslims live outside the Middle East. And yet in the Western imaginary Muslim countries of the Middle East are seen as "the central lands of Islam," just as "Christianity" is usually taken to mean Latin Christianity and does not refer to the important (and continuous) Christian communities in Muslim-majority countries.

11   See John Stuart Mill's "Representative Government," esp. chap. 8 (1861), in *Three Essays* (London, 1973).

12   Zabala, "A Religion Without Theists or Atheists," p. 6.

13   Rorty and Vattimo, *Future of Religion,* p. 72.

14   R. Alta Charo, J.D., "Body of Research—Ownership and Use of Human Tissue," *New England Journal of Medicine* 355 (October 12, 2006).

15   K. J. Dover, "Classical Greek Attitudes to Sexual Behaviour," in Mark Golden and Peter Toohey, eds., *Sex and Difference in Ancient Greece and Rome* (Edinburgh, 2003), pp. 117–18.

16   Mark Rose, "The Author as Proprietor: *Donaldson v. Becket* and the Genealogy of Modern Authorship," *Representations* 23 (Summer 1988).

[17] See Martha Woodmansee, "The Genius and the Copyright: Economic and Legal Conditions of the Emergence of the 'Author,'" *Eighteenth-Century Studies* 17, no. 4 (1984).

[18] Alain Cabantous, *Blasphemy: Impious Speech in the West from the Seventeenth to the Nineteenth Century* (New York, 2002), p. 5.

[19] Hent de Vries has made precisely this argument by drawing on Derrida as well as Benjamin in his excellent *Religion and Violence* (Baltimore, 2002).

[20] W. C. Van Unnik, "The Christian's Freedom of Speech in the New Testament," *Bulletin of the John Rylands Library* 44 (1962): p. 487.

[21] See Joss Marsh, *Word Crimes: Blasphemy, Culture, and Literature in Nineteenth-Century England* (Chicago, 1998). Marsh deals with more than two hundred blasphemy trials, all of which had a strong class component.

[22] See Edward William Lane's *Arabic-English Lexicon* (London, 1863). See also A. de Biberstein Kazimirski's *Dictionnaire Arabe-Français* (Cairo, 1875), which gives "Blasphémer Dieu, et faire nargue de ses bienfaits."

[23] In this respect it overlaps with such words as *shatīma, sabb, istihāna.*

[24] *Bayān al-ittihād hawl nashr suwar masī'a li-rrasūl* (Statement of the [World] Union [of Islamic Scholars] About the Publication of Images Insulting to the Prophet), Cairo, January 23, 2006: www.qaradawi.net/site/topics/article.asp?cu_no=4143&version=1&template_id=116&parent_id=114.

[25] The book that got Nasr Hamid Abu Zayd declared an apostate (and hence no longer legally married to his wife) was *Mafhūm al-nass: Dirāsah fi 'ulūm al-Qur'ān* (Understanding the [sacred] text: A study of the sciences of the Qur'an) (Beirut, 1990). Two interesting articles on Abu Zayd's methodology should be noted: Charles Hirschkind, "Heresy or Hermeneutics: The Case of Nasr Hamid Abu Zayd," *Stanford Humanities Review* 5, no. 1 (1996), and Saba Mahmood, "Secularism, Hermeneutics, and Empire: The Politics of Islamic Reformation," *Public Culture* 18, no. 2 (2006). Mahmood deals with Abu Zayd among other liberal Islamic reformers.

[26] A detailed account of the case is given in Kilian Bälz, "Submitting Faith to Judicial Scrutiny Through the Family Trial: The 'Abu Zayd Case,'" *Die Welt des Islams,* New Series 37, no. 2 (1997). A more interesting account is provided in chap. 1 ("The Legalization of *Hisba* in the Case of Nasr Abu Zayd") of Hussein Agrama's PhD dissertation *Law Courts and Fatwa Councils in Modern Egypt: An Ethnography of Islamic Legal Practice,* The Johns Hopkins University, 2005. Extended extracts from the judgments in the court of first instance, the court of appeals, and the court of cassation, are given (in French translation) in "Jurisprudence Abu Zayd," *Egypte/Monde Arabe,* no. 34 (1998). The original Arabic judgments are contained in Muhammad Salim al-'Awwa, *al-haq fi al-ta'bīr* (The right to free speech), (Cairo, 1998).

[27] Al-'Awwa, *al-haq fi al-ta'bīr,* p. 23. See also Ahmad Rashad Tahun, *Hurriyat al-*

'aqīda fi-shsharī'a al-islāmiyya (Cairo, 1998), who is more concerned with the political issues—especially with the unity of the *umma*—than al-'Awwa is.

[28] In a recent article Baber Johansen has traced Ibn Taymiyya's position on the question of coerced confession. "Whereas the torture of witnesses played an important role in Roman law and in late medieval judicial practice of Europe," Johansen observes, "it is unknown in Muslim legal doctrine." But Ibn Taymiyya took an unusually political view of the law's role, and in so doing advocated the legal admissibility of coerced evidence. See "Signs as Evidence: The Doctrine of Ibn Taymiyya (1263–1328) and Ibn Qayyim Al-Jawziyya (D. 1351) on Proof," *Islamic Law and Society* 9, no. 2 (2002): citation on p. 171.

[29] In "What Is Enlightenment" Kant makes what may appear to be a similar distinction when he speaks about "public" and "private" reason. The latter, however, depends on the concept of the state in relation to which an arena for the conduct of public debate is circumscribed. Al-'Awwa has no such argument. His concern is simply with the representability of personal belief as an inner condition.

[30] "It is to be noted that according to the definition (1) blasphemy is set down as a word, for ordinarily it is expressed in speech, though it may be committed in thought or in act. Being primarily a sin of the tongue, it will be seen to be opposed directly to the religious act of praising God. (2) It is said to be against God, though this may be only mediately, as when the contumelious word is spoken of the saints or of sacred things, because of the relationship they sustain to God and His service"; *The Catholic Encyclopedia* (New York, 1907), 2:595.

[31] Al-'Awwa, *al-haq fi al-ta'bīr*, p.13.

[32] Al-Shaykh 'Uthman Safi, *'Ala Hāmish "Naqd al-fikr ad-dīnī"* (A Footnote to "The Critique of Religious Thought") (Beirut, 1970), p. 87.

[33] Bälz, "Submitting Faith," p. 143.

[34] Johansen, "Signs as Evidence."

[35] See the excellent ethnographic study by Winnifred Fallers Sullivan, *The Impossibility of Religious Freedom* (Princeton, 2005).

[36] Ibid., pp. 12–13.

[37] This is not unlike the premodern meaning of the word "belief" in English and its equivalents in other European languages. See chap. 6 of Wilfred Cantwell Smith, *Faith and Belief* (Oxford, 1998), for an interesting etymology of the word.

[38] There has been considerable disagreement in modern Islamic history over the criteria for determining apostasy, as well as whether, and if so how, it should be punished. Thus one of the medieval collections of *hadith*, by Bukhari, records a statement by the Prophet Muhammad that apostates must be killed; but another canonical collection, that by Muslim, declares

this statement to be inauthentic. The debate has continued in modern times.

39   See the sensitive analysis in Dorothea Weltecke, "Beyond Religion: On the Lack of Belief During the Central and Late Middle Ages," in *Religion and Its Other: Secular and Sacral Concepts and Practices in Interaction*, ed. Jörg Feuchter, Michi Knecht, and Heike Bock (Chicago, 2008).

40   A typical sentence: *wa-l-fitnatu ashaddu min al-qatli* (2:191), "persecution is worse than killing."

41   Susan Mendus, *Toleration and the Limits of Liberalism* (Atlantic Highlands, NJ, 1989).

42   "Here I stand: I can do no other," the words attributed to Luther, were probably never uttered, although they express very well the sentiment of his actual statement at the Diet of Worms. See O. Chadwick, *The Reformation* (Harmondsworth, 1972), p. 56. At any rate, what he said on that famous occasion would have to be described as sincere but inauthentic. This doesn't seem right, however.

43   Edward Said, *The World, the Text, and the Critic* (Boston, 1983), p. 26.

44   Michel Foucault, "What Is Critique," trans. Kevin Paul Geiman, in James Schmidt, ed., *What Is Enlightenment? Eighteenth-Century Answers and Twentieth-Century Questions* (Berkeley, 1996).

45   See Reinhart Koselleck, *Crisis and Critique* (Cambridge, MA, 1988), p. 103 n. 15. My colleague John Wallach informs me: "The verb is *krino*, which could signify 'to separate, to discern, to judge.' Related nouns are *krisis* (turning point—potentially between life and death) and *kriterion*, i.e., means for judging, as well as the designation for a 'judge.' Courts were known as *Dikasteriai*, places where judgments of justice were laid down. Judges on Greek juries were called *dikastai*. The Greek goddess of Justice was Dike. Dike derives from the verb *dikazo*, which signified 'to judge, to decide, to establish as a penalty or judgment.' Some relate it to the verb *deiknumi*, which signifies 'to show, make manifest, prove,' etc. There was no verb equivalent of what English speakers have recently made into a verb (from its origins as a noun), viz. 'critique'"; personal communication. A useful account of the history of the term is available in the entries "Krisis" and "Kritik" in *Geschichtliche Grundbegriffe,* ed. Otto Brunner, Werner Conze, and Reinhart Koselleck (Stuttgart, 1972–).

46   See Michel Foucault, *Fearless Speech* (Los Angeles, 2001), pp. 119–33.

47   See Richard Popkin, *The History of Skepticism*, revised and expanded ed. (New York, 2003), esp. chap. 18.

48   Steven Shapin, *A Social History of Truth: Civility and Science in Seventeenth-Century England* (Chicago, 1994).

49   Later, however, the Communist Party would take up the practice of auto-

critique. The most moving example of this that I know in literature is Arthur Koestler's *Darkness at Noon*, trans. Daphne Hardy (London, 1940).

[50] Karl Popper's *Logic of Scientific Discovery* (London, 1959) is the famous statement of his falsification theory. His *The Poverty of Historicism* (London, 1957) was an influential critique directed at the scientific claims of Marxian historicism.

[51] See note 5.

[52] A mere two weeks before the publication of the cartoons, the Danish newspaper *Politiken* printed an article titled "A profound fear of criticizing Islam," which suggests that white majorities in Europe felt beleaguered by the presence of Muslim minorities. See Randall Hansen, "The Danish Cartoon Controversy: A Defence of Liberal Freedom," *International Migration* 44, no. 5 (2006): p. 8.

Saba Mahmood

Religious Reason and Secular Affect: An Incommensurable Divide?

ANY ACADEMIC DISCUSSION of religion in the present moment must countenance the shrill polemics that have become the hallmark of the subject today. The events of the past decade (including 9/11, the subsequent war on terror, and the rise of religious politics globally) have intensified what was at one point a latent schism between religious and secular worldviews. Writers and scholars from both sides of this schism now posit an incommensurable divide between strong religious beliefs and secular values. Indeed, a series of international events, particularly around Islam, are often seen as further evidence of this incommensurability.

Despite this polarization, more reflective voices in the current debate have tried to show how the religious and the secular are not so much immutable essences or opposed ideologies as they are concepts that gain a particular salience with the emergence of the modern state and attendant politics—concepts that are, furthermore, interdependent and necessarily linked in their mutual transformation and historical emergence. Viewed from this perspective, as a secular rationality has come to define law, statecraft, knowledge production, and economic relations in the modern world, it has also simultaneously transformed the conceptions, ideals, practices, and institutions of religious life. Secularism here is understood not simply as the doctrinal separation of church from state but also as the rearticulation of religion in a manner that is commensurate with modern sensibilities and modes of governance. To rethink the religious is also to rethink the secular and its truth claims, its promise of internal and external goods.

While these analytical reflections have complicated the state of academic debate about the religious and the secular, they are often challenged by scholars who fear that this manner of thinking forestalls effective action against the threat of "religious extremism" that haunts our world today. By historicizing the truth of secular reason and questioning its normative claims, one paves the way for religious fanaticism to take hold of our institutions and society. One finds oneself on a slippery slope of the ever-present dangers of "relativism." Our temporal frame of action requires certainty and judgment rather than critical rethinking of secular goods. This was evident in the debate that unfolded around the banning of the veil in France in 2004, just as it was evident in the justifications surrounding the publication of the Danish cartoons depicting Muhammad in 2005 and 2008:[1] if we do not defend secular values and lifestyles, it is argued, "they" (often Islamic extremists), will take over our liberal freedoms and institutions. In this formulation, the choice is clear: either one is against secular values or for them. A moral impasse, it is asserted, is not resolved through reflection but through a vigorous defense of norms and moral standards that are necessary to secular ways of life and conduct.

In this essay, I would like to question this manner of conceptualizing the conflict between secular necessity and religious threat. To begin with, this dichotomous characterization depends upon a certain definition of "religious extremism," often amassing together a series of practices and images that are said to threaten a secular liberal worldview: from suicide bombers, to veiled women, to angry mobs burning books, to preachers pushing "intelligent design" in schools. Needless to say, this diverse set of images and practices neither emanates from a singular religious logic nor belongs sociologically to a unified political formation. The point I want to stress is that these supposed descriptions of "religious extremism" enfold a set of judgments and evaluations such that to abide by a certain description is also to uphold these judgments. Descriptions of events deemed extremist or politically dangerous are often not only reductive of the events they purport to describe but, more importantly, also premised on normative conceptions of the subject, religion, language, and law that are far more fraught than the call for decisive political action allows.

In what follows I would like to consider these issues through the lens of the Danish cartoon controversy. Public reaction on the part of both Muslims and non-Muslims to the publication of Danish cartoons of Muhammad (initially in 2005 and republished in 2008) is exemplary of the standoff between religious and secular worldviews today—particularly in liberal democratic societies. Following the initial publication of the cartoons, while shrill and incendiary polemics were common to both sides, even the calmer commentators seemed to concur that this was an impasse between the liberal value of freedom of speech and a religious taboo. For some, to accommodate the latter would be to compromise the former, and for others, an accommodation of both was necessary for the preservation of a multicultural and multireligious Europe. Both judgments assume that what is at stake is a moral impasse between what the Muslim minority community considers an act of blasphemy and the non-Muslim majority regards as an exercise of freedom of expression, especially satirical expression, so essential to a liberal society. It is this consensus across opposed camps that I want to unsettle in this essay, calling our attention to normative conceptions enfolded within this assessment about what constitutes religion and proper religious subjectivity in the modern world. I hope to show that to abide by the description that the Danish cartoon controversy exemplified a clash between the principles of blasphemy and freedom of speech is to accept a set of prior judgments about what kind of injury or offence the cartoons caused and how such an injury might be addressed in a liberal democratic society. In part I felt compelled to write this essay because of the immediate resort to juridical language as much by those who opposed the cartoons as by those who sought to justify them across the European and Middle Eastern press. Despite polemical differences, both positions remain rooted in an identity politics (Western versus Islamic) that privileges the state and the law as the ultimate adjudicator of religious difference. In the pages that follow I want to question this assessment and force us to think critically about the ethical and political questions elided in the immediate resort to the law to settle such disputes. In conclusion, I will link my argument to a broader discussion of how we might reflect on the presumed secularity of critique in the academy today.

Blasphemy or Free Speech?

The Muslim reaction to the Danish cartoons depicting the Prophet Muhammad, particularly following the first publication,[2] shook the world. This was in part because of the large demonstrations held in a range of Muslim countries, some of which turned violent, and in part due to the vitriolic reaction Muslim objections to the cartoons provoked among Europeans, many of whom resorted to blatant acts of racism and Islamophobia targeted at European Muslims. Given the passions involved on both sides, it is clear that something quite crucial was at stake in this controversy that invites reflection far deeper than simple claims of civilizational difference and calls for decisive action would allow.

Despite the volume of commentary on the subject, there were two stable poles around which much of the debate over the cartoons coalesced. On the one hand were those who claimed that Muslim outcry had to be disciplined and subjected to protocols of freedom of speech characteristic of liberal democratic societies in which no figure or object, no matter how sacred, might be depicted, caricatured, or satirized. Critics of this position on the other hand claimed that freedom of speech has never simply been a matter of the exercise of rights, but entails civic responsibility so as not to provoke religious or cultural sensitivities, especially in hybrid multicultural societies.[3] These critics charged that European governments employ a double standard when it comes to the treatment of Muslims, since, not only is the desecration of Christian symbols regulated by blasphemy laws in countries like Britain, Austria, Italy, Spain, and Germany,[4] but the media also often makes allowances to accommodate Judeo-Christian sensitivities.[5] Given that most Muslims regard the pictorial depiction of the Prophet as either taboo or blasphemous, these critics attributed the gleeful display and circulation of the cartoons to the Islamophobia sweeping North America and Europe following the events of 9/11.[6] For some, this was reminiscent of the anti-Semitic propaganda leveled at another minority in European history that was also at one time portrayed as a drain on Europe's land and resources.[7]

For many liberals and progressives critical of the Islamophobia sweeping contemporary Europe, Muslim furor over the cartoons posed particular problems. While some of them could see the lurking racism behind the cartoons, it was the *religious* dimension of the Muslim protest that remained troubling. Thus, even when there was recognition that Muslim religious sensibilities were not properly accommodated in Europe, there was nonetheless an *inability* to understand the sense of injury expressed by so many Muslims. The British political critic Tariq Ali exemplified this position in a column he wrote for the *London Review of Books*. Ali frames his remarks by dismissing the claim that Muhammad's pictorial depiction constitutes blasphemy in Islam, since countless images of Muhammad can be found in Islamic manuscripts and on coins across Muslim history. He then goes on to ridicule the anguish expressed by many Muslims on seeing or hearing about these images: "As for religious 'pain,' this is, mercifully, an experience denied unbelievers like myself and felt only by divines from various faiths, who transmit it to their followers, or by politicians in direct contact with the Holy Spirit: Bush, Blair, and Ahmedinejad and, of course, the pope and the grand ayatollah. There are many believers, probably a majority, who remain unaffected by insults from a right-wing Danish paper."[8] In Ali's view, Muslims who express pain upon seeing the Prophet depicted as a terrorist (or hearing about such depictions) are nothing but pawns in the hands of religious and political leaders.

Art Spiegelman expressed a similar bewilderment when he wrote in *Harper's* magazine: "[T]he most baffling aspect of this whole affair is why all the violent demonstrations focused on the dopey cartoons rather than on the truly horrifying torture photos seen regularly on Al Jazeera, on European television, everywhere but in the mainstream media of the United States. Maybe it's because those photos of actual violation don't have the magical aura of things unseen, like the damn cartoons."[9] Such views crystallized the sense that it was a clash between secular liberal values and an irascible religiosity that was at stake in the Danish cartoon controversy. Stanley Fish, in an op-ed for the *New York Times,* echoes this view even as he reverses the judgment. For him, the entire controversy is best understood in terms of a contrast between "their" strongly held religious beliefs and "our" anemic liberal morality, one that requires no strong allegiance beyond the assertion of abstract principles (such as free speech).[10]

I want to argue that framing the issue in this manner must be rethought both for its blindness to the strong moral claims enfolded within the principle of free speech (and its concomitant *indifference* to blasphemy) as well as the normative model of religion it encodes. To understand the affront the cartoons caused within terms of racism alone, or for that matter in terms of Western irreligiosity, is to circumscribe our vocabulary to the limited conceptions of blasphemy and freedom of speech—the two poles that dominated the debate. Both these notions—grounded in juridical notions of rights and state sanction—presuppose a semiotic ideology in which signifiers are arbitrarily linked to concepts, their meaning open to people's reading in accord with a particular code shared between them. What might appear to be a symbol of mirth and merrymaking to some may well be interpreted as blasphemous by others. In what follows, I will suggest that this rather impoverished understanding of images, icons, and signs not only naturalizes a certain concept of a *religious* subject ensconced in a world of encoded meanings but also fails to attend to the affective and embodied practices through which a subject comes to relate to a particular sign—a relation founded not only on representation but also on what I will call attachment and cohabitation. It is striking that the largely silent but peaceful and emphatic rejection of these images among millions of Muslims around the world was so easily assimilated to the language of identity politics, religious fanaticism, and cultural/civilizational difference. Little attention has been paid to how one might reflect on the kind of offence the cartoons caused and what ethical, communicative, and political practices are necessary to make this kind of injury intelligible. The lacuna is all the more puzzling given how complex notions of psychic, bodily, and historical injury now permeate legal and popular discourse in Western liberal societies; consider, for example, the transformations that concepts of property, personal injury, and reparations have undergone in the last century alone.

I want to clarify at the outset (lest I be misunderstood) that my goal here is not to provide a more authoritative model for understanding Muslim anger over the cartoons: indeed, the motivations for the international protests were notoriously heterogeneous, and it is impossible to explain them through a single causal narrative.[11] Instead, my aim in pursuing this line of thinking is to push us to consider why such little thought has been given in academic and public debate to what constitutes moral injury in our secular world today? What are the conditions of intelligibility that render certain moral claims legible and others mute, where the language of street violence can be mapped onto the matrix of racism, blasphemy, and free speech, but the claim to what Tariq Ali pejoratively calls "religious pain" remains elusive, if not incomprehensible? What are the costs entailed in turning to the law or the state to settle such a controversy? How might we draw on the recent scholarship on secularism to complicate what is otherwise a polemical and shrill debate about the proper place of religious symbols in a secular democratic society?

Religion, Image, Language

W. J. T. Mitchell has argued that we need to reckon with images not just as inert objects but also as animated beings that exert a certain force in this world. Mitchell emphasizes that this force should not be reduced to "interpretation" but taken up as a relationship that binds the image to the spectator, object to subject, in a relationship that is transformative of the social context in which it unfolds. He argues: "[T]he complex field of visual reciprocity is not merely a by-product of social reality but actively constitutive of it. Vision is as important as language in mediating social relations, and it is not reducible to language, or sign, or to discourse. Pictures want equal rights with language, not to be turned into language."[12]

Mitchell's insistence that the analysis of images not be modeled on a theory of language or signs is instructive, in that it reminds us that not all semiotic forms follow the logics of meaning, communication, or representation.[13] Yet the idea that the primary function of images, icons, and signs is to communicate meaning (regardless of the structure of relationality in which the object and subject reside) is widely held and was certainly regnant in much of the discourse about the Danish cartoons.[14] Webb Keane, in his recent book *Christian Moderns*, traces the imbricated genealogy of this understanding of semiotic forms and the modern concept of religion.[15] He follows a number of other scholars in pointing out that the modern concept of religion—as a set of propositions in a set of beliefs to which the individual gives assent—owes its emergence to the rise of Protestant Christianity and its subsequent globalization. Whereas colonial missionary movements were the carriers for many of the practical and doctrinal elements of Protestant Christianity to various parts of the world, aspects of Protestant semiotic ideology became embedded in more secular ideas of what it means to be modern. One crucial aspect of this semiotic ideology is the distinction between object and subject, between substance and meaning, signifiers and signified, form and essence.[16] Unglued from its initial moorings in doctrinal and theological concerns, these sets of distinctions have become a part of modern folk understandings of how images and words operate in the world. One version of this is evident in Ferdinand de Saussure's model of language, which posits an immutable distinction between the realm of language and the realm of things (material or conceptual), between the sign and the world, between speech and linguistic system. One finds in Saussure, argues Keane, a preoccupation not entirely different from that which agitated Calvin and other Protestant reformers: how best to institute the distinction between the transcendent world of abstract concepts and ideas and the material reality of this world.

Historical anthropologists have drawn attention to the shock experienced by proselytizing missionaries when they first encountered non-Christian natives who attributed divine agency to material signs, often regarded material objects (and their exchange) as an ontological extension of themselves (thereby dissolving the distinction between persons and things), and for whom linguistic practices did not simply denote reality but also helped create it (as in the use of ritual speech to invoke ancestral spirits or divine presence).[17] The dismay that Protestant Christian missionaries felt at the moral consequences that followed from native epistemological assumptions, I want to suggest, has resonances with the bafflement many liberals and progressives express at the scope and depth of Muslim reaction over the cartoons today.[18] One source of bafflement emanates from the semiotic ideology that underpins their sense that religious symbols and icons are one thing, and sacred figures, with all the devotional respect they might evoke, another. To confuse one with the other is to commit a category mistake and to fail to realize that signs and symbols are only arbitrarily linked to the abstractions that humans have come to revere and regard as sacred. As any modern sensible human being must understand, religious signs—such as the cross—are not embodiments of the divine but only stand in for the divine through an act of human encoding and interpretation. On this reading, Muslims agitated by the cartoons exhibit an improper reading practice, collapsing the necessary distinction between the subject (the divine status attributed to Muhammad) and the object (pictorial depictions of Muhammad). Their agitation, in other words, is a product of a fundamental confusion about the materiality of a particular semiotic form that is only arbitrarily, not necessarily, linked to the abstract character of their religious beliefs.

A critical piece of this semiotic ideology entails the notion that insomuch as religion is primarily about belief in a set of propositions to which one lends one's assent, it is fundamentally a matter of choice. Once the truth of such a conception of religion, and concomitant subjectivity, is conceded, it follows that wrongheaded natives and Muslims can perhaps be persuaded to adopt a different reading practice, one in which images, icons, and signs do not have any spiritual consequences in and of themselves but are only ascribed such a status through a set of human conventions. The transformative power of this vision was precisely what motivated the eighteenth- and nineteenth-century missionaries to undertake the pedagogical project of teaching native subjects to distinguish properly between inanimate objects, humans, and divinity. It is this same vision that seems to inform the well-meaning pleas circulating in Europe today for Muslims to stop taking the Danish cartoons so seriously, to realize that the image (of Muhammad) can produce no real injury given that its true locus is in the interiority of the individual believer and *not* in the fickle world of material symbols and signs. The hope that a correct reading practice can yield compliant subjects crucially depends, in other words, upon a prior agreement about what religion *should* be in the modern world. It is this normative understanding of religion internal to liberalism that is often missed and glossed over by commentators such as Stanley Fish (as in the quote earlier) when they claim that liberalism is anemic in its moral and religious commitments.

Relationality, Subject, and Icon

I want to turn now to a different understanding of icons that not only was operative among Muslims who felt offended by the cartoons but also has a long and rich history within different traditions, including Christianity and ancient Greek thought. A quick word on my use of the term *icon*: it refers not simply to an image but to a cluster of meanings that might suggest a persona, an authoritative presence, or even a shared imagination. In this view, the power of an icon lies in its capacity to allow an individual (or a community) to find oneself in a structure that influences how one conducts oneself in this world. The term *icon* in my discussion therefore pertains not just to images but to a form of relationality that binds the subject to an object or imaginary.

At the time of their initial publication, I was struck by the sense of personal loss expressed by many devout Muslims on hearing about or seeing the cartoons. While many of those I interviewed condemned the violent demonstrations, they nonetheless expressed a sense of grief and sorrow.[19] As one young British Muslim put it:

> I did not like what those raging crowds did in burning down buildings and cars in places like Nigeria and Gaza. But what

really upset me was the absolute lack of understanding on the part of my secular friends (who are by the way not all White, many are from Pakistan and Bangladesh) at how upset people like myself felt on seeing the Prophet insulted in this way. It felt like it was a personal insult! The idea that we should just get over this hurt makes me so mad: if they don't feel offended by how Jesus is presented (and some do of course), why do they expect that all of us should feel the same? The Prophet is not after all Mel Gibson or Brad Pitt, he is the *Prophet*!

When the cartoons were republished in seventeen Danish and a handful of European and American newspapers in February 2008, I was conducting field research in Cairo, Egypt. While the demonstrations were muted this time, I heard similar expressions of hurt, loss, and injury expressed by a variety of people. An older man, in his sixties, said to me: "I would have felt less wounded if the object of ridicule were my own parents. And you know how hard it is to have bad things said about your parents, especially when they are deceased. But to have the Prophet scorned and abused this way, that was too much to bear!"

The relationship of intimacy with the Prophet expressed here has been the subject of many studies by scholars of Islam and is explicitly thematized in Islamic devotional literature on Muhammad and his immediate family *(ahl al-bayt)*.[20] In this literature, Muhammad is regarded as a moral exemplar whose words and deeds are understood not so much as commandments but as ways of inhabiting the world, bodily and ethically. Those who profess love for the Prophet do not simply follow his advice and admonitions to the *umma* (that exist in the form of the *hadith*), but also try to emulate how he dressed; what he ate; how he spoke to his friends and adversaries; how he slept, walked, and so on. These mimetic ways of realizing the Prophet's behavior are lived not as commandments but as virtues where one wants to ingest, as it were, the Prophet's persona into oneself.[21] It needs to be acknowledged of course that insomuch as Muhammad is a human figure in Islamic doctrine who does not share in divine essence, he is more an object of veneration than of worship.[22]

The point I wish to emphasize is that, within traditions of Muslim piety, a devout Muslim's relationship to Muhammad is predicated not so much upon a communicative or representational model as on an assimilative one. Muhammad, in this understanding, is not simply a proper noun referring to a particular historical figure, but the mark of a relation of similitude. In this economy of signification, he is a figure of immanence in his constant exemplariness, and is therefore not a referential sign that stands apart from an essence that it denotes. The modality of attachment that I am describing here (between a devout Muslim and the exemplary figure of Muhammad) is perhaps best captured in Aristotle's notion of *schesis*, which he used to describe different kinds of relations in *Categories*, a concept that was later elaborated by the Neoplatonists (such as Porphyry, Ammonius, and Elias).[23] The *Oxford English Dictionary* defines *schesis* as "the manner in which a thing is related to something else." Scholars commenting on Aristotle's use of *schesis* distinguish it from his use of the term *pros ti* in that *schesis* captures a sense of embodied habitation and intimate proximity that imbues such a relation. Its closest cognate in Greek is *hexis* and in Latin *habitus,* both suggesting a bodily condition or temperament that undergirds a particular modality of relation.

Particularly relevant to my argument here is the meaning *schesis* was given during the second iconoclastic controversy (circa 787) when, perhaps not surprisingly, it was the iconophiles who used it to respond *against* charges of idolatry and to defend their doctrine of consubstantiality. Kenneth Parry, in his book on Byzantine iconophile thought, shows that Aristotle's concept of relationality became crucial to the defense of the holy image by the two great iconophiles, Theodore of Studite and the Patriarch Nikephoros.[24] As Parry shows, what the image and the prototype share in their discourse is not an essence (human or divine) but the relationship between them. This relationship is based in homonymy and hypostasis: the image and deity are two in nature and essence but identical in name. It is the imaginal structure shared between them that gives form to this relationship. In the words of the historian Marie-José Mondzain, "to be the 'image of' is to be in a living relation to."[25] The Aristotelian term *schesis* captures this living relation because of its heightened psychophysiological and emotional connotations and its emphasis on familiarity and intimacy as a necessary aspect of the relation.

What interests me in this iconophile tradition is not so much the image as the concept of relationality that binds the subject to the object of veneration. This modality of relationship is operative in a number of traditions of worship and often coexists in some tension with other dominant ideologies of perception and religious practice.[26] The three Abrahamic faiths adopted a range of key Aristotelian and Platonic concepts and practices that were often historically modified to fit the theological and doctrinal requirements of each tradition.[27] In contemporary Islam, these ideas and practices, far from becoming extinct, have been reconfigured under conditions of new perceptual regimes and modes of governance—a reconfiguration that requires serious engagement with the historical relevance of these practices in the present.[28]

Schesis aptly captures not only how a devout Muslim's relationship to Muhammed is described in Islamic devotional literature but also how it is lived and practiced in various parts of the Muslim world. Even the thoroughly standardized canon of the *Sunna* (an authoritative record of the Prophet's actions and speech) vacillates between what read like straightforward commands, on the one hand, and descriptions of the Prophet's behavior, on the other, his persona and habits understood as exemplars for the constitution of one's own ethical and affective equipment. For many pious Muslims, these embodied practices and virtues provide the substrate through which one comes to acquire a devoted and pious disposition. Such an inhabitation of the model (as the term *schesis* suggests) is the result of a labor of love in which one is bound to the authorial figure through a sense of intimacy and desire. It is not due to the compulsion of "the law" that one emulates the Prophet's conduct, therefore, but because of the ethical capacities one has developed that incline one to behave in a certain way.

The sense of moral injury that emanates from such a relationship between the ethical subject and the figure of exemplarity (such as Muhammad) is quite distinct from one that the notion of blasphemy encodes. The notion of moral injury I am describing no doubt entails a sense of violation, but this violation emanates not from the judgment that "the law" has been transgressed but from the perception that one's being, grounded as it is in a relationship of dependency with the Prophet, has been shaken. For many Muslims, the offense the cartoons committed was not against a moral interdiction ("Thou shalt not make images of Muhammad"), but against a structure of affect, a habitus, that feels wounded. This wound requires moral action, but its language is neither juridical nor that of street protest, because it does not belong to an economy of blame, accountability, and reparations. The action that it requires is internal to the structure of affect, relations, and virtues that predisposes one to experience an act as a violation in the first place.

One might ask what happens to this mode of injury when it is subject to the language of law, politics, and street protest? What are its conditions of intelligibility in a world where identity politics reign and the juridical language of rights dominates? Does it remain mute and unintelligible or does its logic undergo a transformation? How does this kind of religious offence complicate principles of free speech and freedom of religion espoused by liberal democratic societies?

Religion, Race, and Hate Speech

An unfortunate consequence of assessing the cartoon controversy in terms of blasphemy and freedom of speech was the immediate resort to juridical language by participants on both sides. In what follows, I want to examine two distinct arguments mobilized by European Muslims in order to seek protection from what they regard as increasing attacks on their religious and cultural identity: first, the use of European hate speech laws and, second, the legal precedents set by the European Court of Human Rights (ECtHR) to limit free speech in the interest of maintaining social order. These attempts, as I will show, encounter strong challenges not simply because of the European majority's prejudice against Muslims but because of structural constraints internal to secular liberal law, its definition of what religion is, and its ineluctable sensitivity to majoritarian cultural sensibilities.

According to many European Muslims, the cartoons are a particularly vicious example of the racism they have come to experience from their compatriots in Europe. As Tariq Modood put it: "The cartoons are not just about one individual Muslim per se—just as a cartoon about Moses as a crooked financier would not be about one man but a comment on Jews. And just as the latter would be racist, so are the cartoons in question."[29] Modood mobilizes this provocative, if somewhat simplified, comparison with European Jews to challenge the idea regnant among many Europeans—progressives and conservatives alike—that Muslims cannot be subjected to racism because they are a religious, not a racial, group. Modood argues that racism is not simply about biology but can also be directed at culturally and religiously marked groups. Once we move away from a biological notion of race, it is possible to see that "Muslims can [also] be the victims of racism qua Muslims as well as qua Asians or Arabs or Bosnians. Indeed...these different kinds of racisms can interact...and so can mutate and new forms of racism can emerge. This is...to recognize that a form of racism has emerged which connects with but goes beyond a critique of Islam as a religion."[30] While Modood does not adequately address the distinct histories of racialization of European Jews and Muslims, his viewpoint nonetheless enjoys wide support among many people.

Arguments about the racialization of Muslims provoke the fear among some Europeans that if this premise is conceded or accorded legal recognition then it will open the door for Muslims to use European hate speech laws to unduly regulate forms of speech that they think are injurious to their religious sensibilities.[31] Ardent champions of free speech often reject the claim that the Danish cartoons have anything to do with racism or Islamophobia, arguing instead that Muslim extremists are using this language for their own nefarious purposes. A number of legal critics, for example, charge that Muslim use of European hate speech laws is a ruse by "opponents of liberal values" who understand that "in order to be admitted into the democratic debate, they [have] to use a rhetoric that hides the conflict between their ideas and the basic tenets of open societies."[32] These voices caution softhearted liberals and multiculturalists not to fall for such an opportunistic misuse of antidiscrimination and human rights discourse because, they warn ominously, it will lead to the enforcement of "Islamic values" and the ultimate destruction of the "Europe of the Enlightenment."[33]

This rejection of Muslim invocations of hate speech laws turns upon two arguments: (a) religious identity is categorically different from racial identity, and (b) evidence of racial discrimination against Muslims in European societies is lacking. In regard to the former, these critics argue that race is an immutable biological characteristic, whereas religion is a matter of choice. One can change one's religion but not one's skin color. The Danish cartoons, on the other hand, merely offended "religious belief."[34] According to the legal critic Guy Haarscher, insomuch as racist behavior refuses to grant equal status to Jews and blacks "because of their [perceived] biologically 'inferior' character," it violates the liberal principle of equality. "Blasphemy," on the other hand, he asserts "is normal—and maybe a cathartic value—in open societies."[35]

What I want to problematize here is the presumption that religion is ultimately a matter of choice: such a judgment is predicated on a prior notion, one I mentioned earlier, that religion is ultimately about belief in a set of propositions to which one gives one's assent. Once this premise is granted, it is easy to assert that one can change one's beliefs just as easily as one might change one's dietary preferences or one's name. While the problematic conception of race as a biological attribute might be apparent to the reader, the normative conception of religion offered here encounters few challenges.[36] Earlier I explicated the concomitant semiotic ideology this conception encodes; here I want to draw out the implications of this concept when it is encoded within secular liberal understandings of injurious speech and the right to freedom of expression. The legal critics I cite do not simply misrecognize the kind of religiosity at stake in Muslim reactions to Danish cartoons: they also echo the presumptions of the civil law tradition in which the epistemological status of religious belief has come to be cast as speculative and therefore less "real" than the materiality of race and biology. Notably, in the arguments I cited earlier, the normative conception of religion as belief facilitates other claims about what counts as evidence, materiality, and real versus psychic or imagined harm.

In a thoughtful article entitled "The Limits of Toleration" Kirstie McClure shows how the idea that religion is primarily about private belief is closely tied to the historical emergence of the notion of "worldly harm" in the eighteenth century when the modern state came to extend its jurisdiction over a range of bodily practices (both religious and nonreligious) deemed pertinent to the smooth functioning of the newly emergent civic domain. As a result, a variety of religious rituals and practices (such as animal sacrifice) had to be made inconsequential to religious doctrine in order to bring them under the purview of civil law. This in turn depended upon securing a new epistemological basis for religion and its various doctrinal claims on subjects, space, and time. McClure shows, for example, that the argument for religious toleration in John Locke's *A Letter Concerning Toleration* is grounded in an empiricist epistemology that empowers the state "as the sole legitimate adjudicator of worldly practice. The boundaries of toleration… [come] to be civilly defined...by the empirical determination of whether particular acts and practices are demonstrably injurious to *the safety and security of the state or the civil interests of its citizens,* with these latter defined in equally empirical terms."[37] There is little doubt that since the time of Locke the notion of harm has been considerably expanded beyond the narrow confines of this empiricist conception, but the idea that religion is about matters less material (and therefore less pressing) continues to hold sway in liberal societies. This claim paradoxically provokes contemporary defenders of religion to try to ground its truth in empirical proofs, thereby constantly reinscribing the empiricist epistemology that was germane to Locke's regime of civic order.

McClure's argument draws attention to the ways in which the emergence of the modern concept of religion is intrinsically tied to the problem of governance and statecraft. In the debate about the Danish cartoons, the limits of toleration were quickly set by concerns for "the safety and security of the state." The Muslim charge that the cartoons were racist was often dismissed as nothing but an expression of "fundamentalist Islam," and it was not long before Muslim criticisms of the cartoons came to be regarded as a threat not simply to the civilizational essence of Europe but also to European state security and public order. Legal critics like András Sajó insist, for example, that to accept the charge that the Danish cartoons are racist is to ignore the real danger of Islamic terrorism that the cartoons highlight: "[T]he cartoons indicate a truly unpleasant *factual* connection...between terrorism and one very successful version of Islam....If every critical expression becomes suspicious of the danger of generalization..., [then] this will lead to self-censure....If the criticism of religion is successfully recategorized as racism, then that means. . . that you cannot criticize religious terrorism, even though religion *really* does have its finger in the terrorism pie."[38]

It is striking that in casting the matter as a choice between Islamic terrorism and open debate, Sajó, like many others, portrays the cartoons as statements of facts that are necessary to the security and well-being of liberal democracies.[39] The performative aspect of the Danish cartoons is ceded in favor of their informational content, reducing them to little more than referential discourse. Not only does this view naturalize a language ideology in which the primary task of signs is the communication of referential meaning but it also construes all those who would question such an understanding as religious extremists or, at the very least, as soft multiculturalists who do not fully comprehend the threat posed to liberal democracy by Islam. Furthermore, insomuch as this juridical logic requires clear and distinct categories (such as religion versus race), it leaves little room for understanding ways of being and acting that cut across such distinctions. When concern for state security is coupled with this propensity of positive law, it is not surprising that Muslim recourse to European hate speech laws is judged as spurious.

Religion, Law, and Public Order

For European Muslims, a second plausible legal option to pursue is the precedent set by the ECtHR when it upheld two state bans on films deemed offensive to Christian sensibilities. The European Convention for the Protection of Human Rights (ECHR) is modeled after the Universal Declaration of Human Rights, but, unlike the latter, it has the power to implement decisions on member states of the Council of Europe. Two recent decisions of ECtHR are of relevance here: the *Otto-Preminger-Institut v. Austria* ruling in 1994 and the *Wingrove v. United Kingdom* judgment in 1997, both of which banned the display and circulation of films for offending devout Christians. It is important to point out that these decisions were grounded not in European blasphemy laws but in article 10 of the convention, which ensures the right to freedom of expression. Notably, while article 10(1) of the ECHR holds "freedom of expression" to be an absolute right, article 10(2) allows for the exercise of this right to be limited if the restrictions are prescribed by law and are understood to be necessary to the functioning of a democratic society.[40] It is important to note that this regulated conception of freedom of expression in Europe stands in sharp contrast with the more libertarian conception of free speech in the United States. Most European countries, coming out of the experience of the Holocaust and the Second World War, place strong restrictions on forms of speech that might foster racial hatred and lead to violence.

At stake in the *Otto-Preminger-Institut v. Austria* case was a film produced by the nonprofit Otto Preminger Institute that portrayed God, Jesus, and Mary in ways that were offensive to Christian sensibilities.[41] Under section 188 of the Austrian Penal Code, the film was seized and confiscated before it could be shown.[42] The filmmaker appealed the case to the ECtHR, which ruled in favor of the Austrian government and did not find the government in violation of ECHR article 10. The Austrian government had defended the seizure of the film "in view of its character as an attack on the Christian religion, especially Roman Catholicism.... Furthermore, they [the Austrian government] stressed the role of religion in the everyday life of the people of Tyrol [the town where the film was to be shown]. The proportion of Roman Catholic believers among the Austrian population as a whole was already considerable—78%—among Tyroleans it was as high as 87%. Consequently...there was a pressing social need for the preservation of religious peace; it had been necessary to protect public order against the film."[43] The ECtHR concurred with this judgment and argued: "The Court cannot disregard the fact that the Roman

Catholic religion is the religion of the overwhelming majority of the Tyroleans. In seizing the film, the Austrian authorities acted to ensure religious peace in that region and to prevent that some people should feel the object of attacks on their religious beliefs in an unwarranted and offensive manner."[44]

A similar regard for Christian sensibilities informed the ECtHR's decision in the *Wingrove v. United Kingdom* case when the court upheld the British government's refusal to permit circulation of a film found to be offensive to devout Christians. The ECtHR made clear that, while it found the British blasphemy laws objectionable, it supported the decision of the government in this instance on the basis of the state's margin of appreciation for permissible restrictions operative in article 10 of the ECHR. The court upheld the government's decision to withhold circulation of the film because it had a legitimate aim to "protect the right of others" and to protect "against seriously offensive attacks on matters regarded as sacred by Christians."[45]

While these decisions of the European Court have been criticized for accommodating religious feelings at the cost of free speech, I would like to draw attention to a different issue, namely, the margin of appreciation accorded to the state in determining when and how free speech may be limited. The second clause of article 10 of the ECHR on free speech gives the state a wide margin of appreciation to limit free speech if the state deems it a threat to "national security, territorial integrity, public safety, health and morals of a society, or reputations and rights of others." In commenting upon the centrality of the concept of "public order" undergirding this legal tradition, Hussein Agrama argues that it is part of a broader semantic and conceptual field in which notions of public health and morals and national security are interlinked, and the referent almost always seems to be the majority religious culture.[46] A fundamental contradiction haunts liberal democratic legal traditions, he argues; on the one hand everyone is "equal before the law," and, on the other, the aim of the law is to create and maintain public order—an aim that necessarily turns upon the concerns and attitudes of its majority population.[47]

While some European Muslims see ECtHR judgments as blatantly hypocritical (they accommodate Christian sensitivities but ignore Muslims ones), I would like to point out that regardless of the social context when this legal reasoning is used, it tends to privilege the cultural and religious beliefs of the majority population. A number of observers of the ECtHR have noted, for example, that "there appears to be a bias in the jurisprudence of the Court...toward protecting traditional and established religions and a corresponding insensitivity towards the rights of minority, nontraditional, or unpopular religious groups....[T]hose religions established within a state, either because they are an official religion or have a large number of adherents, are more likely to have their core doctrines recognized as manifestations of religious belief."[48] It is not surprising, therefore, that when the majority religion was Islam, as in the *I. A. v. Turkey* (2005) case, the ECtHR ruling was consistent with the reasoning used in the *Otto-Preminger-Institut* and the *Wingrove* decisions. The ECtHR upheld the Turkish government's ban on a book deemed offensive to the majority Muslim population on the basis that it violated the rights of others who were offended by its profaneness; as such, the Turkish government's decision had met a "pressing social need" and was not in violation of article 10 of the ECtHR.

The ECtHR is not the only legal institution where state concern for security and public and moral order leads to the accommodation of majority religious traditions. Consider, for example, the much publicized apostasy trial of Nasr Hamid Abu Zayd in Egypt.[49] Abu Zayd was tried for the crime of apostasy on the basis of his published academic writings. The case was introduced and tried based on a religious principle called *hisba* that did not exist in modern Egyptian legal codes before 1980 but was adopted in the litigation process expressly to declare Abu Zayd an apostate. Agrama, in his incisive analysis of this trial, shows that while the principle of *hisba* existed historically in classical Sharia, the form it took in the Abu Zayd case differed dramatically in that it came to be articulated with the concept of public order and the state's duty to uphold the morals of the society in congruence with the Islamic tradition of the majority. The language Agrama analyzes from the Abu Zayd case bears striking similarities with invocations of public order in the ECtHR decisions cited earlier. Despite the different sociopolitical contexts, what is shared between the Egyptian legal arguments and those of the ECtHR is the French legal tradition's concern for public order and, by extension, the law's privileging of majority religious sensibilities.

It might be argued that the *Otto-Preminger-Insitut* and the Abu Zayd cases abrogate the secular liberal principle of state neutrality by accommodating the sensitivities of a religious tradition.[50] But such an objection, I would suggest, is based on an erroneous understanding of liberal secularism as abstaining from the domain of religious life. As much of recent scholarship suggests, contrary to the ideological self-understanding of secularism (as the doctrinal separation of religion and state), secularism has historically entailed the regulation and reformation of religious beliefs, doctrines, and practices to yield a particular normative conception of religion (that is largely Protestant Christian in its contours). Historically speaking, the secular state has not simply cordoned off religion from its regulatory ambitions but sought to remake it through the agency of the law. This remaking is shot through with tensions and paradoxes that cannot simply be attributed to the intransigency of religionists (Muslims or Christians). One particular tension is manifest in how freedom of religion often conflicts with the principle of freedom of speech, both of which are upheld by secular liberal democratic societies.[51] As might be clear to the reader, the contradictions I have discussed here are not simply the result of the machinations of opportunistic religious extremists or an ineffective secular state but are at the heart of the legal and cultural organization of secular societies. To attend to these contradictions is to admit to the shifting nature of secularism itself and the problems it historically manifests.

Moral Injury and Requirements of the Law

In light of my argument in the first part of this essay, it is important to note how far this juridical language of hate speech and religious freedom has come from the kind of moral injury I discussed under the concept of *schesis*. Muslims who want to turn this form of injury into a litigable crime must reckon with the performative character of the law. To subject an injury predicated upon distinctly different conceptions of the subject, religiosity, harm, and semiosis to the logic of civil law is to promulgate its demise (rather than to protect it). Mechanisms of the law are not neutral but are encoded with an entire set of cultural and epistemological presuppositions that are not indifferent to how religion is practiced and experienced in different traditions. Muslims committed to preserving an imaginary in which their relation to the prophet is based on similitude and cohabitation must contend with the transformative power of the law and disciplines of subjectivity on which the law rests.

What I want to emphasize here is that European Muslims who want to lay claim to the language of public order (enshrined in the recent ECtHR decisions) remain blind to this normative disposition of secular-liberal law to majority culture. In its concern for public order and safety, the sensitivities and traditions of a religious minority are deemed necessarily less weighty than those of the majority, even in matters of religious freedoms. This is not simply an expression of cultural prejudice; it is constitutive of the jurisprudential tradition in which the right to free speech and religious liberty is located (and to which European Muslims are now increasingly turning for protection). Furthermore, insomuch as Muslims have come to be perceived as a threat to state security, their religious traditions and practices are necessarily subject to the surveillance and regulatory ambitions of the state in which the language of public order reigns supreme.

For anyone interested in fostering greater understanding across lines of religious difference it would be important to turn not so much to the law as to the thick texture and traditions of ethical and intersubjective norms that provide the substrate for legal arguments (enshrined in the language of public order). In this essay, I have suggested several reasons why the concept of moral injury I have analyzed here remained unintelligible in the public debate over the Danish cartoons, particularly the difficulties entailed in translating across different semiotic and ethical norms. The future of the Muslim minority in Euro-American societies is often posed as a choice between assimilation and marginalization. In this matrix of choice, the question of translatability of practices and norms across semiotic and ethical differences is seldom raised. I read this elision not as an epistemological problem but in terms of the differential of power characteristic of minority-majority relations within the context of nation-states. It might well be that, given this differential, the Muslim minority in Europe will have no choice but to assimilate. For those who are interested in other ways of dealing with this problem, however, it may behoove us to avoid the rush to judgment so as to begin to unravel the different stakes in such stand-offs. Ultimately, the future of the Muslim minority in Europe depends not so much on how secular-liberal protocols of free speech might be expanded to accommodate its concerns as on a larger transformation of the cultural and ethical sensibilities of the Judeo-Christian population that undergird the cultural practices of secular-liberal law.[52] For a variety of historical and sociological reasons, I am not sure if either the Muslim immigrant community or the European majority is prepared for such an undertaking.

Conclusion

Rather than reiterate my main arguments, I would like to close by offering some thoughts on how my analysis bears upon the exercise of critique—a rubric under which this essay might be located and that characterizes what most academic work labors to achieve. It is customary these days to tout critique as an achievement of secular culture and thought. Key to this coupling is the sense that unlike religious belief, critique is predicated upon a necessary distantiation between the subject and object and some form of reasoned deliberation. This understanding of critique is often counterposed to religious reading practices where the subject is understood to be so mired in the object that she cannot achieve the distance necessary for the practice of critique. In a provocative essay, Michael Warner argues that such a conception of critique not only caricatures the religious Other but also, more importantly, remains blind to its own disciplines of subjectivity, affective attachments, and subject-object relationality.[53] He tracks some of the historical transformations (in practices of reading, exegesis, entexualization, and codex formation) that constitute the backdrop for the emergence of this regnant conception of critique. Warner urges readers to recognize and appreciate the disciplinary labor that goes into the production of a historically peculiar subjectivity entailed in this conception of critique.

In this essay, I have tried to pull apart some of the assumptions that secure the polarization between religious extremism and secular freedom wherein the former is judged to be uncritical, violent, and tyrannical and the latter tolerant, satirical, and democratic. My attempt is to show that to subscribe to such a description of events is also simultaneously to underwrite a problematic set of notions about religion, perception, language, and, perhaps more importantly, in an increasingly litigious world, what law's proper role should be in securing religious freedom. I hope it is clear from my arguments that the secular liberal principles of freedom of religion and speech are not neutral mechanisms for the negotiation of religious difference and that they remain quite partial to certain normative conceptions of religion, subject, language, and injury. This is not due to a secular malfeasance but to a necessary effect that follows from the layers of epistemological, religious, and linguistic commitments built into the matrix of the civil law tradition. Our ability to think outside this set of limitations necessarily requires the labor of critique, a labor that rests not on its putative claims to moral or epistemological superiority but in its ability to recognize and parochialize its own affective commitments that contribute to the problem in various ways.

Insomuch as the tradition of critical theory is infused with a suspicion, if not dismissal, of religion's metaphysical and epistemological commitments, it would behoove us to think "critically" about this dismissal: how are epistemology and critique related within this tradition? Do distinct traditions of critique require a particular epistemology and ontological presuppositions of the subject? How might we rethink the dominant conception of time—as empty, homogenous, and unbounded, one so germane to our conception of history—in light of other ways of relating to and experiencing time that also suffuse modern life? What are some of the practices of self-cultivation—including practices of reading, contemplation, engagement, and sociality—internal to secular conceptions of critique? What is the morphology of these practices and how do these sit with (or differ from) other practices of ethical self-cultivation that might uphold contrastive notions of critique and criticism?

The kind of labor involved in answering these questions requires not simply posing a "yes" or a "no" answer to the query "Is Critique Secular?" To do so would be to foreclose thought and to fail to engage a rich set of questions, answers to which remain unclear, not because of some intellectual confusion or incomplete evidence, but because these questions require a comparative dialogue across the putative divide between "Western" and "non-Western" traditions of critique and practice. This dialogue in turn depends on making a distinction between the labor entailed in the analysis of a phenomenon and defending our own beliefs in certain secular conceptions of liberty and attachment. The tension between the two is a productive one for the exercise of critique insomuch as it suspends the closure necessary to political action so as to allow thinking to proceed in unaccustomed ways. The academy, I believe, remains one of the few places where such tensions can still be explored.

An earlier version of this essay appeared in Critical Inquiry *35 no. 4 (2009). I would like to thank the University of Chicago Press for their permission to reprint the article. I am grateful to Charles Hirschkind, Hussein Agrama, Talal Asad, and Michael Allan for their comments. I am particularly indebted to Amy Russel for guiding me through Greek sources on* schesis *and relationality, and I am grateful to Mark McGrath for providing research assistance beyond the call of duty. The essay was presented at the University of Chicago, Columbia University, New York University, and the Social Science Research Council's forum on secularism, whose audiences I thank for their comments and provocations.*

Endnotes

[1]   The French government banned the veil as well as the display of other "conspicuous" religious symbols from state schools in 2004. For historical background and debates about this decision, see Joan Scott, *The Politics of the Veil* (Princeton, NJ, 2007). For the Danish cartoons, see note 2.

[2]   The cartoons were initially published in *Jyllands-Posten* in September 2005. Large protests within the Muslim world broke out in 2006. The reasons for these protests were diverse, and many critics claimed they were opportunistically exploited by Muslim governments for their own ends. On February 13, 2008, *Jyllands-Posten* and many other Danish newspapers, including *Politiken and Berlingske Tidende*, reprinted the infamous *Bomb in the Turban* cartoon as a statement of "commitment to freedom of speech." Several newspapers in Europe and the U.S. followed suit, some of which had initially refused to publish them. The newspapers claimed this was in reaction to the reported arrest of three men of North African descent who were allegedly plotting to kill the cartoonist Kurt Westergaard. One of the two was released for lack of evidence and the other two, nonresidents of Denmark, were deported to Tunisia. The reaction to the republication of the cartoons among Muslims was muted this time, according to reports, and most demonstrations remained peaceful.

[3]   For two different examples of this position, see Jospeh Carens's essay "Free Speech and Democratic Norms in the Danish Cartoon Controversy" in the special issue of *International Migration*, "The Danish Cartoon Affair: Free Speech, Racism, Islamism, and Integration," 44, no. 5 (2006): pp. 33–42; and Tariq Ramadan, "Cartoon Controversy Is Not a Matter of Freedom of Speech, but Civic Responsibility," *New Perspectives Quarterly*, February 2, 2006, http://www.digitalnpq.org/articles/global/56/02-02-2006/tariq_ramadan. Also see Tariq Ramadan, "Cartoon Conflicts," *Guardian*, February 6, 2006, http://www.guardian.

co.uk/cartoonprotests/story/0,,1703496,00.html.

4   Among the European countries in which blasphemy laws still exist on
    the books (even if they are infrequently used) are Austria, Denmark,
    Germany, Greece, Iceland, Finland, The Netherlands, Spain, Italy,
    Switzerland, and the United Kingdom.

5   For example, shortly after the protests erupted over the Danish cartoons,
    the British *Guardian* reported that *Jyllands-Posten* (the same newspaper
    that had solicited the Muhammad cartoons) had refused to publish
    drawings mocking Jesus Christ for fear of provoking "an outcry" among
    Danish Christians; http://www.guardian.co.uk/media/2006/feb/06/
    pressandpublishing.politics.

6   See, for example, Tariq Modood's essays in the special issue of
    International Migration, "The Danish Cartoon Affair: Free Speech, Racism,
    Islamism, and Integration": "The Liberal Dilemma: Integration or
    Vilification?" pp. 4–7, and "Obstacles to Multicultural Integration," pp.
    51–61.

7   As one British Muslim critic put it, there are strong parallels between
    how Muslims are characterized in Europe today and how the Jews were
    characterized in the 1930s: as religious bigots, aliens, and a blight on
    European civilization. See Maleiha Malik, "Muslims Are Getting the
    Same Treatment Jews Had a Century Ago," *Guardian*, February 2, 2007.
    See http://www.guardian.co.uk/commentisfree/story/0,,2004258,00.
    html.

8   Tariq Ali, "LRB Diary," *London Review of Books* 28, no. 5 (March 9, 2006).
    See http://www.tariqali.org/LRBdiary.html.

9   Art Spiegelman, "Drawing Blood: Outrageous Cartoons and the Art of
    Courage," *Harper's* 312, no. 1873 (June 2006): p. 47.

10 According to Fish, liberal morality "consists in a withdrawal from
    morality in any strong, insistent form," such that liberals do not
    care whether their beliefs prevail or not. Muslims, on the other
    hand, have strong beliefs (however misguided they may be) whose
    implementation they regard crucial. Stanley Fish, "Our Faith
    in Letting It All Hang Out" *New York Times*, February 12, 2006;
    http://www.nytimes.com/2006/02/12/opinion/12fish.html?_
    r=1&pagewanted=all&oref=slogin. Fish's view is problematic on a
    number of accounts. First, liberalism enfolds a conception of religiosity
    that is not simply negative in its formulation but has a robust sense and
    feel that is manifest in the place accorded to religious myths, texts, icons,
    and symbols in the cultural and literary resources of liberal societies.
    Charles Taylor's recent book *A Secular Age* (Cambridge, MA, 2007)
    provides a rich account of this form of religiosity, one to which Fish
    remains blind. Second, Fish characterizes both free speech and religion
    as belief systems, with one difference: the former is weak whereas the

latter is passionately embraced. It is important to note that neither the liberal nor the Islamic tradition is merely about belief: each is about practices, how subjects come to be attached to authoritative ideas, images, icons, and sensibilities. It is because of this rather impoverished view of liberal ideology that Fish does not appreciate the strong and visceral reactions among secular liberal Europeans against Muslim protests.

11 For a critical review of the contrasting motivations behind the protests staged in a number of Muslim countries, see Mahmood Mamdani, "The Political Uses of Free Speech," *Daily Times* (Lahore), Feburary 17, 2006, http://www.dailytimes.com.pk/default.asp?page=2006%5C02%5C17%5 Cstory_17-2-2006_pg3_3.

12 W. J. T. Mitchell, *What Do Pictures Want? The Lives and Loves of Images* (Chicago, 2005), p. 47.

13 Mitchell devotes an entire chapter to the analysis of "offending images" that have been desecrated by spectators, such as Chris Ofili's painting *The Holy Virgin Mary,* which was displayed in the Brooklyn Museum of Art. Mitchell argues that such images are distinct in that they are "transparently and immediately linked to what [they] represent... [S]econd...the image possesses a kind of vital, living character that makes it capable of feeling what is done to it. It is not merely a transparent medium for communicating a message but something like an animated, living thing, an object with feelings, intentions, desires and agency. Indeed images are sometimes treated as pseudopersons—not merely as sentient creatures that can feel pain and pleasure but as responsible and responsive social beings. Images of this sort seem to look back at us, to speak to us, even to be capable of suffering harm or of magically transmitting harm when violence is done to them"; ibid., p. 127.

14 Needless to say that such an understanding of language has been challenged and complicated by a number of linguists and philosophers. For an insightful discussion, see Benjamin Lee, *Talking Heads: Language, Metalanguage, and the Semiotics of Subjectivity* (Durham, NC, 1997).

15 Webb Keane, *Christian Moderns: Freedom and Fetish in the Mission Encounter* (Berkeley, CA, 2007).

16 These sets of distinctions are predicated on a distantiation between the perceiving subject and the world of objects, a distantiation that many scholars consider a distinguishing feature of modernity. Keane draws upon the work of Timothy Mitchell, *Colonizing Egypt* (Berkeley, CA, 1991), and Bruno Latour, *We Have Never Been Modern* (Cambridge, MA, 2007) to make this point.

17 See Keane's discussion of this point in chap. 8 of *Christian Moderns*; also see Webb Keane, "Freedom and Blasphemy: On Indonesian Press Bans

and Danish Cartoons," *Public Culture* 21, no. 1 (2009): pp. 47–76. For earlier debates, see Jean Comaroff and John Comaroff, *Of Revelation and Revolution* (Chicago, 1991); Marcel Mauss, *The Gift: The Form and Reason for Exchange in Archaic Societies* (New York, 2008); Peter Pels, *Politics of Presence* (New York, 1998).

[18] The moral outrage expressed by Muslims was not that dissimilar to the anger and passion defenders of free speech exhibited; the appellation "fundamentalists" for the Muslim protesters encodes the judgment that the protestors are backward and regressive demagogues distinct from principled supporters of freedom of speech.

[19] While violent demonstrations and the boycott of Danish products caught the attention of the world, a far more widespread form of Muslim dissent was hardly mentioned. In Egypt, for example, this consisted of long evenings of worship dedicated to the memory of Muhammad in mosques, and the widespread use of the slogan *"Ihna fidak ya rasul allah!"* meaning "We would die for you O prophet of God!" The expression *"fidak"* is often used to express feelings of ardor and love toward one's beloved and in Sufi discourse also expresses one's adoration of God. This particular phrase was popularized by an Egyptian soccer player, pride of the national team, when, during a soccer match, he bared his t-shirt imprinted with this phrase unexpectedly to the media. Henceforth, it caught on like wildfire and was reportedly displayed in offices; on vehicles, computer screens, and t-shirts; and adapted as a ring tone for mobile phones. Many of those who adopted this form of "silent protest," when interviewed, strongly rejected the violence of demonstrations in Nigeria, Pakistan, and Gaza—but nonetheless expressed pain, hurt, and anger at the images.

[20] For an examination of both historical and contemporary relevance of this relation to popular culture, see Ali Asaani, *Celebrating Muhammad: Images of the Prophet in Popular Muslim Poetry* (Columbia, SC, 1995).

[21] The tradition of virtue ethics, which draws on key Aristotelian conceptions, forms part of the discourse of piety in contemporary Islam. This tradition has been resuscitated by the Islamic revival in a variety of contexts—including the media but also in practices of the self. On this, see my *Politics of Piety: The Islamic Revival and the Feminist Subject* (Princeton, NJ, 2005).

[22] Within Christianity, the way Mary is venerated marks the distinction between the divinity of Jesus and the humanness of Mary.

[23] In his commentary on Aristotle's *Categories*, Ammonius distinguishes between four types of *schesis*: relationship between master and disciple; between master and slave; between parent and child; and between lovers. The term is also relevant to the Stoic concept and practice of "cultivation of character." See Marie-José Mondzain, "Voir L'invisible,"

Critique 42, no. 589–90 (June/July 1996).

24   Parry identifies Aristotle's *Categories* and Porphyry's *Isagoge*—neither of which were used before in defense of the holy image—as crucial to the arguments of later iconophiles. Kenneth Parry, *Depicting the Word: Byzantine Iconophile Thought of the Eighth and Ninth Centuries* (Leiden, 1996); see esp. chap. 6, "Aristotelianism."

25   Marie-José Mondzain, *Image, Icon, Economy: Byzantine Origins of the Contemporary Image* (Stanford, CA, 2004). Mondzain quotes the patriarch Nikephoros's defense against the charge of consubstantiality through his recourse to arguments about art: "Art imitates nature without the former being identical with the latter. On the contrary, having taken the natural visible form as a model and as a prototype, art makes something similar and alike.... It would be necessary then, according to this argument, that the man and his icon share the same definition and be related to each other as consubstantial things" (p. 77).

26   Christopher Pinney's work on the political effects of the all-pervasive presence of the images of Hindu icons, gods, and deities in India is an instructive place to think through some of these issues. See Christopher Pinney, *Photos of the Gods: The Printed Image and Political Struggle in India* (New York, 2004).

27   The historical trajectory of these ideas is interesting to trace in this regard. Notably, it was the school at Alexandria that proved to be the most important transmitter of Aristotle's works to the Byzantines. When the school at Athens was closed under Justinian in the sixth century, it was the Alexandria school that continued to flourish first under Christian and then Islamic influence up until the eighth century. Many of the inheritors of this school of commentators ended up in Baghdad, which became a center of Neoplatonist thought in the ninth century. See Parry, *Depicting the Word*, p. 53; and Richard Sorabji, "Aristotle Commentators," http://www.muslimphilosophy.com/ip/rep/A021.htm.

28   On this point, see Charles Hirschkind, *The Ethical Soundscape* (New York, 2006); particularly the discussion about subterranean perceptual regimes and modern conditions of politics and media.

29   Modood, "The Liberal Dilemma," p. 4.

30   Modood, "Obstacles to Multicultural Integration," p. 57.

31   For example, Muslim associations in France unsuccessfully sought to use antihate speech legislation against the French newspaper *France-Soir* that republished the cartoons in support of *Jyllands-Posten*.

32   Guy Haarscher "Free Speech, Religion, and the Right to Caricature," in *Censorial Sensitivities: Free Speech and Religion in a Fundamentalist World*, ed. A. Sajó (Utrecht, 2007), p. 313.

33   András Sajó, "Countervailing Duties as Applied to Danish Cheese and

Danish Cartoons," in Sajó, *Censorial Sensitivities*, p. 299.

34 Sajó argues, "Undoubtedly, the negative stereotyping of group members plays an important role in racist parlance. The Danish cartoons, however, addressed a religious belief. On what ground can you equate unchangeable race (skin color) and religion, if religion is a matter of choice?" ibid., p. 286.

35 Haarscher, "Free Speech," p. 323.

36 The strict distinction drawn here between religious and racial identity is put into question by the gradual shift in the European understanding of Jews from a religious group to a racial people over the course of the twentieth century. For an interesting argument about how the "racialization of Jews" in Europe came to be historically linked with the construction of Arabs as quintessentially religious/Muslim, see Gil Anidjar, *Semites: Race, Religion, Literature* (Stanford, CA, 2008).

37 Kirstie McClure, "Limits to Toleration," *Political Theory* 18 no. 3 (1990): p. 380–81 (emphasis added).

38 Sajó, *Censorial Sensitivities*, p. 288 (emphasis added).

39 American legal critic Robert Post expresses a similar view when he argues: "Some of the cartoons do invoke stereotypic criticisms of Islam. They comment on Islamic repression of women; on the use of Islamic fundamentalist doctrines to foster violence; on the fear of violent reprisal for publishing criticism of Islam. These are ideas that have been and will be used by those who would discriminate against Muslims.... *But they are also ideas about real and pressing issues.* The relationship between Islam and gender is a lively and controversial question. Fundamental Islamic violence is a public worry throughout Europe. Fear of reprisal for crossing Islamic taboos is omnipresent.... *To cut off all public discussion of real and pressing public issues would be unthinkable.* And if such issues are to be discussed, the expression of all relevant views must be protected," in "Religion and Freedom of Speech: Portraits of Muhammad," *Constellations* 14 no. 1 (2007): pp. 83–84 (emphasis added). This article was republished in Sajó, *Censorial Sensitivities.* For my response to this piece, see http://townsendcenter.berkeley.edu/pubs/post_mahmood.pdf.

40 Article 10(1) states: "Everyone has the right to freedom of expression. This right shall include freedom to hold opinions and to receive and impart information and ideas without interference by public authority and regardless of frontiers. This article shall not prevent States from requiring the licensing of broadcasting, television or cinema enterprises." Article 10(2) allows for permissible limits in the following manner: "The exercise of these freedoms, since it carries with it duties and responsibilities, may be subject to such formalities, conditions, restrictions or penalties as are prescribed by law and are necessary in a democratic society, in the interests of national security, territorial

integrity or public safety, for the prevention of disorder or crime, for the protection of health or morals, for the protection of the reputation or rights of others, for preventing the disclosure of information received in confidence, or for maintaining the authority and impartiality of the judiciary." See, http://www.hrcr.org/docs/Eur_Convention/euroconv3.html.

[41]   Not unlike the publishers of the Danish cartoons, the filmmaker argued that it was doubtful that "a work of art dealing in a satirical way with persons or objects of religious venerations could ever be regarded as 'disparaging or insulting,'" *Otto-Preminger-Institut v. Austria Judgment, Eur. H. R. Rep.* 19 (1994) §44.

[42]   The Austrian government maintained that the seizure and confiscation of the film was aimed at the "protection of the rights of others," particularly the right to respect for one's religious feelings, and at the "prevention of disorder"; ibid., §46. Also see Peter Edge, "The European Court of Human Rights and Religious Rights," *International and Comparative Law Quarterly* 47 no. 3 (July 1998): pp. 680–87; and Javier Martinez-Torrón and Rafael Navarro-Valls, "The Protection of Religious Freedom in the System of the European Convention on Human Rights," *Helsinki Monitor* no. 3 (1998): pp. 25–37.

[43]   *Otto-Preminger-Institut v. Austria Judgment* §52.

[44]   Ibid. §56.

[45]   *Wingrove v. United Kingdom Judgment, Eur. H. R. Rep.* 19 (1996) §57.

[46]   See Hussein Agrama, "Egypt: A Secular or a Religious State?" (PhD diss., Johns Hopkins University, 2005).

[47]   Hussein Agrama, "Is Egypt a Religious or a Secular State? Reflections on Islam, Secularism, and Conflict," manuscript, forthcoming in *Comparative Studies in Society and History* (2009): p. 15.

[48]   Peter Danchin, "Of Prophets and Proselytes: Freedom of Religion and the Conflict of Rights in International Law," *Harvard International Law Journal* 49 no. 2 (Summer 2008): p. 275. Danchin cites a number of critics of ECtHR judgments who hold this view, including Jeremy Gunn, "Adjudicating Rights of Conscience Under European Convention on Human Rights," *Religious Human Rights in Global Perspective: Legal Perspectives*, ed. J. van der Vyver and J. Witte (The Hague, 1996).

[49]   It is important to note that while the category of apostasy was used in Islamic legal tradition until the twelfth century, apostasy trials had practically disappeared in the Middle East between 1883 and 1950. It is only in the 1980s that apostasy emerges as a litigable crime for the first time in the modern Middle Eastern history of the penal code. Baber Johansen shows that it was not until the 1980s, under increasing demand for the codification of Islamic law *(taqnin al-sharia)*, that classical notions of apostasy came to be integrated into the penal code in a number of

countries such as the Sudan (1991), Yemen (1994), and Egypt (1982). Insomuch as the Sharia only applies to matters of Personal Status Law, it is through this channel that apostasy has reentered the legal system in Egypt. Baber Johansen, "Apostasy in Egypt," *Social Research* 70, no. 3 (2003): pp. 687–710.

[50] Indeed, this is the basis on which a number of legal theorists objected to the ECtHR's decision. See for example, Sajó, *Censorial Sensitivities,* and Martinez-Torrón and Navarro-Valls, "The Protection of Religious Freedom in the System of the European Convention on Human Rights."

[51] While my argument here focuses on the French legal tradition, a similar tension haunts the American tradition as well. Winnifred Sullivan explores the paradoxical implications of the First Amendment (particularly the freedom of religion clause) in the legal history of the United States. She analyzes a representative court case in Florida in which a municipal authority was sued on First Amendment grounds for banning display of religious symbols in a public cemetery. In adjudicating this case, the court had ultimately to distinguish and decide which of the religious beliefs claimed by the litigants were real from the standpoint of the law. In doing so, the federal court had to engage in theological reasoning and judgments, an exercise that sharply contradicts the principle of state neutrality with respect to religion enshrined in the First Amendment; see Winnifred Sullivan, *The Impossibility of Religious Freedom* (Princeton, NJ, 2005). There are other examples in U.S. legal history, such as the Supreme Court ruling that banned the use of peyote in ceremonial rituals of the Native American Church. On that case, see Vine Deloria and David Wilkins, *Tribes, Treaties, and Constitutional Tribulations* (Austin, TX, 1999).

[52] Here I am reminded of the fact that the relative abatement of racist attitudes against Jews and blacks in Europe and the United States is not an achievement of the law alone (although the law helped), but crucially depended upon the transformation of the dense fabric of ethical and cultural sensibilities across lines of racial and religious difference.

[53] Michael Warner, "Uncritical Reading," in *Polemic: Critical or Uncritical,* ed. Jane Gallop (New York, 2004), pp. 13–37.

Judith Butler

The Sensibility of Critique:
Response to Asad and Mahmood

ONE MIGHT EXPECT THAT a volume centrally engaged with the events of the Danish cartoon affair and its aftermath would move directly to the normative questions of whether the cartoons constituted a substantial injury, whether those who crafted and published the cartoons were rightfully exercising their freedom of speech, and whether the offense of religious sensibilities ought rightly to be prohibited. Much ink has been spilled on these issues, but little attention has been paid to the question of why outrage against the cartoons by Muslim populations across the globe was of a certain kind, and of what specific meaning that injury had and has. To say that vast populations were injured, or understood themselves as injured, as a consequence of these public displays, however, is still not to say anything about how that injury ought to be addressed or redressed. But it does point to a certain limit of the normative imagination when it is constrained by established juridical protocols on free speech. If one objects to learning about the meaning of the injury at issue because one fears that such an understanding will directly imply a legal proscription of speech, then one embraces a certain norm at the expense of understanding itself—an anti-intellectualism that characterizes forms of moral dogmatism, whether secular or religious. Not only would one prefer to remain ignorant, but one embraces one's ignorance in the name of unyielding moral principles—a comic and tragic position, to be sure.

The two papers featured here petition us to approach the question of blasphemy and injury in another way. They explicitly query whether the available juridical frameworks (deemed "secular" and "liberal" by both authors) that establish the normative questions, is this free speech? and ought it to be protected? are the right ones for understanding what has happened here and what its meaning and importance may be. Of course, to query the adequacy of that framework is not to say this is not free speech and ought not to be protected, since that judgment stays within the same juridical framework—although there will be those who think that any position that refuses to answer these normative questions regarding justification and prohibition is sidestepping the main questions of the day. But such critics have effectively decided that there is but one normative framework within which to understand and evaluate this phenomenon, and that the phenomenon is presumptively understood well by that framework.[1] Those who work within the presumption of a single and adequate framework make all kinds of suppositions about the cultural sufficiency and breadth of their own thought. As a result, they will doubtless think that the refusal to accept this monolithic framework (secular, legal) is nothing but a covert way of taking up—and disavowing—a position *within* that framework. Such reasoning confirms the monolithic hegemony of the framework. However, it remains indifferent to questions of social history and cultural complexity that reframe the very character of the phenomenon in question. Such critics presume that the normative juridical framework within which they work is, and must be, not just predominant, but the necessary way to understand the meaning of events.

It may seem that the problem, as outlined, depends on a distinction between the "meaning" of the events and the "normative evaluation" of those events (justified/unjustified; permissible/impermissible). I am not always sure how Talal Asad and Saba Mahmood would negotiate this distinction, and it does seem that sometimes they direct us to try to understand the meaning of the injury at issue and to suspend the question of evaluation, or "judgment."

I would like to suggest, however, that something more far-reaching is at issue here, since, depending on which normative framework controls the semantic field, the phenomenon in question will turn out to be a different sort of thing. In other words, we can choose to locate the meaning of "blasphemy" within Christian discourse and social history, or as a problem produced by the emergence of free speech doctrine in the last few centuries of European and American legal history. We refer to those frameworks in order to locate the phenomenon, and those frameworks are for the most part normative, addressing the question of whether or not blasphemy is, and ought to be, permitted speech; whether it tests the limits of free speech; and whether its permissibility is a sign of the robust condition of free speech in any given society. If we are asked instead to understand how blasphemy and injury function within Muslim religious law and its history, then we are immediately up against a problem of translation: not only the problem of whether the injury of the Danish cartoons is rightly translated by *tajdīf* or *isā'ah* but also of whether the moral framework and discourse within which the outrage took place was not in some key ways at odds with the moral framework and discourse that for the most part controls the semantic operation of "blasphemy" as a term. The translation has to take place within divergent frames of moral evaluation. Indeed, one of the points of these essays is to show that in some ways the conflict that emerged in the wake of the publication of the Danish cartoons is one between competing moral frameworks, understanding "blasphemy" as a tense and overdetermined site for the convergence of differing schemes of moral evaluation.

Of course, to suggest that there may be other normative frameworks for understanding the problem of blasphemy or offense is not the same as saying that one ought to adopt those other frameworks or that those frameworks ought now to become the ones within which normative judgments are made. And yet, it would not make sense to say that description and prescription are absolutely distinct enterprises. The point is that when we judge, we locate the phenomenon we judge within a given framework, and our judgment requires a stabilization of the phenomenon. But if that stabilization proves impossible, or if the phenomenon—in this case, blasphemy—exists precisely at the crossroads of competing, overlapping, interruptive, and divergent moral frameworks, then we need first to ask ourselves why we locate it within the singular framework that we do, and at what expense we rule out the competing or alternative frameworks within which it is figured and circulated. The point is not simply to expand our capacities for description or to assert the plurality of frameworks, although it is doubtless a "good" to know the cultural range of moral discourses on such questions if we are to be thoughtful and knowledgeable about the world in which we live. Nor is the point to embrace a cultural relativism that would attribute equivalence to all moral claims and position oneself as an outsider to the normative issues at hand. Rather, it seems most important to ask, what would judgment look like that took place not "within" one framework or another but which emerged at the very site of conflict, clash, divergence, overlapping? It would seem a practice of cultural translation would be a condition of such judgment, and that what is being judged is not only the question of whether a given action is injurious but also whether, if it is, legal remedies are the best way to approach the issue, and what other ways of acknowledging and repairing injury are available.

In my view, the point is to achieve a complex and comparative understanding of various moral discourses, not only to see why we *evaluate* (and value) certain norms as we do, but also to evaluate those very modes of evaluation. We do not merely shift from an evaluative position to a descriptive one (though I can see why taking a descriptive tone might work to defuse polemics on all sides), but rather seek to show that every description is already committed to an evaluative framework, prior to the question of any explicit or posterior judgment. We may think that we first describe a phenomenon and then later subject it to judgment, but if the very phenomenon at issue only "exists" within certain evaluative frameworks, then norms precede description—as is surely the case when we think about the presumptive cultural and moral frameworks brought to bear on the discussions of blasphemy against Muhammad as well as those frameworks, mainly Muslim, that were *not* brought to bear. In this instance, the point is to try to clarify why so many Muslims were outraged, and why something other than an attack on free speech by religious populations was at issue. These two anthropologists are trying to get us to expand our understanding of what was at stake, but I gather they are doing this because they think not just that we should all become more knowledgeable (and that broader knowledge of our world is a moral good) but also that the secular terms should not have the power to define the meaning or effect of religious concepts. This is an important argument to make in order to combat a kind of structural injury, emblematized by events like the Danish cartoons, inflicted on religious and racial minorities (especially when religious minorities are racialized).

This last is a strong normative claim, and I want to suggest that it becomes possible to consider the injustice of this situation of hegemonic secularism only when we pass through a certain displacement of taken-for-granted modes of moral evaluation, including certain established juridical frameworks. A certain critical perspective emerges as a consequence of comparative work. An inquiry that understands that competing and converging moral discourses require a mode of cultural analysis, perhaps anthropological, affirms cultural difference as a constant point of reference in the effort to "parochialize" certain absolutist and monolithic conceptions of normativity that serve, implicitly or explicitly, forms of cultural ignorance, racism, conquest, and domination— or, as Asad puts it, the "European revulsion against Muslim immigrants and Islam."[2]

IN A SEPARATE CONTEXT, I have sought to make the case for Asad's normative commitments, despite his very interesting and confounding protestations to the contrary.[3] My position is probably not one that either Mahmood or Asad would embrace in the forms I have offered previously or now, but it is nevertheless one that I could not have undertaken without the benefit of their work. Consider the effect of Asad's injunction to establish a comparative framework for thinking about why we respond to violence as we do, with what affect, and with what sorts of moral evaluations. In *On Suicide Bombing,* he asks why death dealing on the part of nonstate actors fills most people in the "West" with greater horror than death dealing on the part of recognized nation-states. He writes explicitly:

> I am not interested here in the question, "When are particular acts of violence to be condemned as evil, and what are the moral limits to justified counter-violence." I am trying to think instead about the following question: "What does the adoption of particular definitions of death dealing do to military conduct in the world?"[4]

Clearly, we want to know what adopting certain definitions of death dealing does to military conduct not because we are simply purveyors of military landscapes. Presumably, we want to know about these differential ways of defining and experiencing death dealing because they are consequential for why and how wars are waged, and we are trying to shed light on these differential modes in order, in whatever way, to counter and undo them with the hope of ending or ameliorating such wars. And we want to end them, if we do, because we think they are wrong, unjust, contemporary forms of conquest, racist and destructive. All of these are "sentiments" or "affects" that are bound up with our criticism of the differential way in which death dealing is defined and lived.

Asad effectively poses the question, why is it that aggression in the name of God shocks secular liberal sensibilities, whereas the art of killing in the name of the secular nation, or democracy, does not? He points out that this kind of discrepancy or schism may well constitute a "tension" at the heart of the modern subject. And this is a useful and persuasive argument, in my view. But clearly something more is at stake.

We would not be alarmed by the kinds of comparisons made explicit in Asad's questions if we did not ourselves undergo some moral horror or shock at the obvious inequalities demonstrated by the comparison. Asad's questions derive their rhetorical force from a sense that it is unacceptable to respond with righteous outrage to deaths caused by those who wage war in the name of religion and with moral complacency to deaths caused by those who wage war in the name of the nation-state. There are many reasons why one might oppose various forms of death dealing, but *it is only on the condition that we do, in fact, oppose violence and the differential ways it is justified that we can come to understand the normative importance of the comparative judgment that Asad's work makes available to us.* In my view, Asad's work not only provides new modes of description and understanding but also makes an intervention into evaluative frameworks and norms of evaluation themselves. By showing how normative dispositions (mainly secular and liberal) enter into stipulative claims (concerning objectionable violence and grievable death) that circumscribe the domain of "understanding" contemporary cultural and military conflict, Asad facilitates a *critique* of this parochial and consequential circumscription of operative evaluative frameworks. Through a certain kind of comparative interrogation, one framework is interrupted by another, and thus opens up a new horizon for judgment. On the basis of this comparative and interruptive work, we can conclude that there is no reason to assume that justified violence, when it happens, is the sole prerogative of states, and that unjustified violence, when it happens, is the exercise of illegitimate states and insurgency movements. Such a conclusion not only has consequences for how we proceed normatively but also constitutes itself as a strong normative claim.

If Asad's comparative questions upset us, as I think they do, that is because we become aware of the contingent conditions under which we feel shock, outrage, and moral revulsion. And since we can only make sense of why we would feel so much more horror in the face of one mode of death dealing than in the face of another through recourse to implicitly racist and civilizational schemes organizing and sustaining affect differentially, we end up feeling shocked and outraged by our lack of shock. The posing of the comparative question, under the right conditions, induces new moral sentiments that are bound up with new moral judgments. We realize that we have already judged or evaluated the worth of certain lives over others, certain modes of death dealing over others, and that realization is at the same time a judgment, an evaluation, namely, that such differential judgments are unjustified and wrong.

Criticism, Critique, and Formations of the Subject

Asad himself would seem not to agree with the conclusions I derive from his mode of analysis, but perhaps I am offering him a gift he will come to appreciate. Some reflections on "critique" and "criticism" inaugurate and end the essay he offers here. As Wendy Brown has pointed out in the introduction to this volume, the distinction between "critique" and "criticism" is an important one. I would gloss that distinction in the following way: Criticism usually takes an object, and critique is concerned to identify the conditions of possibility under which a domain of objects appears. And although this latter seems like a Kantian definition, it is a Kantianism that has been rewrought several times in the last few centuries with consequences for global politics within and outside the Euro-Atlantic.

As for criticism, consider the difference between Asad's characterization and that, for instance, of Raymond Williams in *Keywords*.[5] After querying whether "criticism signifies liberation," Asad writes, "Let's bear in mind that the term 'criticism' embraces a multitude of activities. To judge, to censure, to reproach, to find fault, to mock, to evaluate, to construe, to diagnose—each of these critical actions relates persons to one another in a variety of affective ways. Thus to be 'criticizable' is to be part of an asymmetrical relation....One should be skeptical, therefore, of the claim that 'criticism' is aligned in any simple way with 'freedom.'"[6]

Williams offers a very different formulation, noting that criticism has been unfairly restricted to "fault-finding" and calling for a way of describing our responses to cultural works "which do not assume the habit (or right or duty) of judgment... [W]hat always needs to be understood is the specificity of the response, which is not a judgment, but a practice" (76). Adorno as well makes clear that judgment of an instrumental kind ought not to be the exemplary act of critique, since the point is not to decide under what category a phenomenon belongs, but to interrogate the taken-for-granted categorical schemes through which phenomena appear. In other words, for Williams and Adorno both (and we might include Deleuze's infamous "having done with judgment" as well), critique does not depend "on a variety of taken-for-granted understandings and abilities"[7]—a position that would, among other things, seem to presume secular understandings as the precondition of its "Western" operation. Indeed, many theorists of critique have rejected judgment as its defining gesture, a trend reversed by the late political philosophy of Hannah Arendt, who seeks recourse to Kant's aesthetic judgment as a model for politics.[8]

Later, in relation to blasphemy, Asad remarks, "[T]he worldly critic wants to see and hear everything: nothing is taboo, everything is subject to critical engagement."[9] Is criticism here the same as critique? If it is, it clearly enjoys a bad reputation as a random, negative, destructive, and judgmental operation. But is this really necessary or, indeed, warranted? Asad cites Said on the notion of the "secular critic," but does this view of criticism really extend adequately to the task of critique, a term that Said himself eschewed? I won't belabor the point here, but consider just a few more formulations that would seem to position critique not only as affectively invested but also as potentially quite powerful in bringing out the secular presuppositions of modern criticism.

Over and against the notion that the worldly critic wants to see and hear everything and subject everything to critical engagement, Gayatri Chakravorty Spivak suggests that we can only subject to "critique" that which we need in order to live. Notice her insistence on this when she considers the stakes of the critique of essentialism: "Deconstruction, whatever it may be, is not most valuably an exposure of error, certainly not other people's error, other people's essentialism. The most serious critique in deconstruction is the critique of things that are extremely useful, things without which we cannot live on, take chances."[10] So here "critique" is bound up with survival, with living on. Although formulated first in relation to the literary arts, Walter Benjamin distinguishes commentary (the object of the critic) from critique by claiming that "critique seeks the truth content of a work of art; commentary, its material content."[11] He explains further that "truth content is bound up with its material content" and that those "works that prove enduring are precisely those whose truth is most deeply sunken in their material content, [and] then, in the course of this duration, the concrete realities rise up before the eyes of the beholder all the more distinctly the more they die out in the world." Obviously not drawing on secular sources,

Benjamin's idea of critique is articulated through metaphors of burial and animation that are as anachronistic as they are true: "If...one views the growing work as a burning funeral pyre, then the commentator stands before it like a chemist, the critic *(Kritiker)* like an alchemist"(298). This last sense of "critic" aligns more closely with critique. This operation is hardly an incessant and random practice of destruction; it is an effort to derive temporality and truth from the material dimension of a work: "[E]very contemporary critique comprehends in the work the moving truth," one that is fossilized or, indeed, crystallized by the force of "progress." For Benjamin, the principles of homogeneity, substitutability, and continuity that come to structure temporality and matter under conditions of capitalism have to be actively interrupted by the way in which the premodern erupts into the modern. Would this notion of critique not be useful to those who seek to show how the progressive conceits of secularization are confounded by animated anachronisms, fragments from the premodern that disrupt the claims of modernity, and prove central— and potentially fatal—to its operation?

Clearly taking his distance from Enlightenment presumptions, Benjamin's ideas of both criticism and critique draw upon a concept of temporality strongly informed by notions of messianic time (which is less a future time, conceived chronologically, than "another time" by which the present is "shot through").[12] But surely, one might respond, some positions on critique derived from Kant, for instance, participate in more complicit ways with the project of secularization. In the history of the Kantian influence on contemporary notions of critique that Asad provides, the legacy of Hermann Cohen and the Marburg School is left to the side, although that reading of Kant laid the groundwork for the critical projects of both Benjamin and Derrida.[13] Nevertheless, let us briefly consider the more difficult case, namely, Foucault, who would seem, according to Asad, not only to situate critique in the tradition of Enlightenment but also to move toward a heroic conception that Asad opposes.

Asad makes the following two central claims about Foucault's essay "What Is Enlightenment?" a text that, in conjunction with "What Is Critique?" offers a way to understand Foucault in light of the Kantian legacy.[14] The first claim is that "Foucault seeks to equate critique with the Kantian notion of Enlightenment." The second is more speculative. He writes, "[T]here is the insistent demand [within modern life] that reasons be given for almost everything. The relation to knowledge, to action, and to other persons *that results when this demand is taken as the foundation of all understanding* is perhaps what Foucault had in mind when he spoke of critique."

My sense is that both of these claims are not quite right. In the first instance, Foucault never "equates" critique with Kantian Enlightenment. In fact, in asking "what is Enlightenment?" Foucault re-poses verbatim the title of Kant's small essay, a mimetic display that calls to be read. Why does Foucault repeat the title? What difference takes place between the first and second iteration? And what is the significance of the question form? It turns out that, for Foucault, enlightenment is not a place or time, but, in Kant's words, "a way out."[15] So already Foucault breaks with a certain historical sequence that would consider the Enlightenment a distinct period of European history. It is a way out, but a way out of what? Is Foucault claiming that Kant provides a way out, or is Foucault, through his very citation of Kant, seeking to establish a way out of Kant? Part of Foucault's brief essay rehearses the Kantian position, to be sure, but perhaps most significant is the moment in which Foucault clearly breaks with Kant's notion that "reason" is the substance of critique. Although Foucault attributes to Enlightenment the injunction, "dare to know," he clearly takes distance from the idea that knowledge is an exclusive function of reason. Foucault exposes the contradictory character of public reason in Kant, since only in relation to public authorities is one authorized to deploy the critical use of reason. The private remains immune from such criticism. So can the recourse to "reason" work at all, if it continually founders on this assumption (one that we can also call "Protestant")? For Kant, it is the use of reason that determines the appropriate conditions under which to accept law and governance, to ascertain what can be known, what must be done, and what may be hoped. But for Foucault, as we know from *The Order of Things* and his criticisms of the Frankfurt School, there is no singular "reason" but orders of rationality, regimes that succeed and converge with one another. Although that is not the point Foucault makes here, it is clear that he breaks with the Kantian exposition in the midst of this essay. Indeed, the break happens rather abruptly when Foucault turns from Kant to Baudelaire. If critique is incessant and does not stop happening, then critique can turn on the concept of reason itself. Indeed, Foucault characterizes the operation of critique in modernity as an "attitude" and an "ethos"—a notion that comes close to the idea of "sensibility" that informs the work of Asad, Mahmood, and the anthropologist Charles Hirschkind.[16]

So, in the first instance, Foucault takes distance from any Enlightenment concept of progress as well as any idea of history that would periodize the Enlightenment as part of a successive chronology of European history. Second, by insisting that critique is an "attitude," Foucault breaks with the Kantian claim that critique belongs to the regime of reason. By "attitude," Foucault means a mode of relating to reality or, alternatively, an ethos—a way of acting and behaving that belongs to a certain culture or community, that signals that belongingness, and that is also an ongoing process and which presents itself as an obligation and a task. The sign of modernity, for Foucault, is to be found neither in the constitutive role of reason in human deliberation nor in the acceptance of existential transience. Rather, it is to "take oneself as object of a complex and difficult elaboration" (311) and to "adopt...a certain attitude with respect to this movement."

At the end of this essay, which poses or, rather, re-poses the question of Enlightenment, Foucault's own relation to the Kantian tradition proves to be complex. Although the tone of this piece is not particularly aggressive or negative, the indebtedness is finally one from which he breaks. True, he relies on Kant, derives some of his vocabulary from Kant, departs from Kant, and remakes Kant, showing only that Kant's text is useful for him. But, in the end, he is refusing the language of adherence and rejection. His argument, he tells us, "does not mean that one has to be 'for' or 'against' the Enlightenment" (313).

If we return to Asad's remark that criticism invariably relies on taken-for-granted schemes of evaluation, we can see that, for Foucault, critique neither destroys the inheritance of thought nor affirms it unequivocally. I note that Asad points out that Islamic jurists working within the Sharia tradition "adopt the principle of epistemological skepticism" (ironic, indeed, when contrasted with first amendment absolutists). In this context, could we say there might be a convergence with the sensibility of Foucault?

In "What Is Critique?" the task of critique is precisely to call into question established frameworks of evaluation—a position that would clearly have strong resonance for a critique of secularism. Moreover, critique does not return us to already established frameworks and norms, but constitutes "a means for a future or a truth that it will not know nor happen to be, it oversees a domain it would not want to police and is unable to regulate."[17] As a mode of living and even a mode of subject constitution, critique is understood as a "practice" that incorporates norms into the very formation of the subject. The subject does not own itself, but is always dispossessed by the norms by which it is formed. Is this conception of no use to the critique of secular presumptions?

IF CRITIQUE WITHIN MODERN critical theory requires the object whose conditions of possibility it seeks to know (Spivak), or stands in an alchemical relation to the object to which it is related (Benjamin), or is finally an "attitude" and "ethos" (Foucault), then perhaps it is not primarily or fundamentally about judgment. Even in Kant, it is important to note that critique is not precisely a judgment, but an inquiry into the conditions of possibility that make judgment possible. That inquiry is, and must be, separate from judgment itself. The Kantian position is that our ways of knowing are structured prior to the possibility of our judgment, and that these form conditions of possibility for any judgment. Kant, of course, sought to understand the universal and timeless features of cognition in his effort to articulate the preconditions of judgment, but it is surely possible to transpose a Kantian procedure onto a historical scheme, as Foucault sought to do. When that happens we can ask, how is our knowledge organized *by specific historical schemes* prior to any possibility of judgment, and how do our judgments rely upon those prior organizations of knowledge? If this is right, and if this constitutes a certain historical transposition of the Kantian project of "critique," then critique would be an inquiry into the ways that knowledge is organized prior to the specific acts of knowledge we perform, including the kinds of judgments we make.

In this sense, following Kant, critique is prior to judgment and perhaps closer to Asad's project than would at first appear. We could say that critique delimits conditions of possibility for knowledge and judgment, but even that would perhaps be too definitive. When we ask what historically formed schemes of evaluation condition and inform our shock and outrage over suicide bombing and our righteous coldness in the face of state-sponsored violence, it seems to me that we are trying to delimit the historical conditions of possibility for affective and evaluative response. Asad and Mahmood both have tried to show how secularism functions tacitly to structure and organize our moral responses within a dominant Euro-Atlantic context, and in so doing they seem to be asking us to call into question the taken-for-granted ways that such schemes inform and move us. Comparative work, perhaps anthropology itself, seeks to displace us from that taken-for-granted set of presumptions, ones that assume a certain process of secularization as yielding universal truths, and that therefore parochialize a very specific, sometimes lethal, tradition within the West.

It seems to me that critique designates the process of trying to delimit knowledge, indicating not so much a completed or successful action as an ongoing task to fathom and describe the various ways of organizing knowledge that are tacitly operating as the preconditions of various "acts" of knowledge. This incomplete effort to delimit and name the conditions of possibility is not itself a judgment; it is an effort to fathom, collect, and identify that upon which we depend when we claim to know anything at all. The ways to do this are various: through tracing internal contradictions, through comparing and contrasting alternative cultural lexicons for similar concepts, through offering a historical account of how a set of culturally specific assumptions became recast as universal and postcultural. If this is one set of critical practices, how different is "critique" from Asad's own critical procedure, finally?

Blasphemy and Self-Ownership

Asad makes clear at the outset of his paper that he is offering "neither an apologia for Muslim reactions to the cartoons "nor a criticism of" those who defended the publication. In the place of apologia and critique, he seeks to "treat [blasphemy] as the crystallization of some moral and political problems in liberal Europe." Blasphemy is viewed in secular liberal society as a constraint on free speech, but why is it contextualized exclusively in this way? Is it that the normative question of whether or not we will censor drives from the start the way in which we conceptualize the phenomenon? If we were to conceptualize the phenomenon differently, would different kinds of normative issues come to the fore?

Of the questions Asad poses about blasphemy, the following seems to be among the most central: Is there an idea of the human implied by prohibitions and protections related to speech, and if so, how does this idea serve to distinguish between what is called the religious and what is called the secular? Asad considers that we take for granted that law functions to protect and prohibit certain kinds of speech, but that we fail to recognize the way in which a given legal system also establishes or produces what will qualify as "free speech." It is not that people are speaking freely (in a prelegal state), and then law comes along, after the fact of free speech, to decide which speech ought to be protected and which speech not. The law does not arrive first and foremost as an adjudicator of already existing speech. Asad points out, for instance, that "copyright is not simply a constraint on free communication but also a way of defining how, when, and for whom literary communication... can be regarded as free, creative, and inalienable." Rather, free speech is produced precisely through the circumscription of the public domain and its protections and, most importantly, it is presumed to belong to a subject who exercises free speech as a right. This subject owns itself and its free speech, and it exercises speech freely as a "property" of its own personhood.[18] As self-owning, the subject possesses its own personhood and exercises that personhood freely; free speech is a paradigmatic example of this self-owning subject. In this way, the claims to free speech are embedded in a certain ontology of the subject, and it is this ontology that is challenged by theological claims that assert the subject or self's dependence on or participation in a transcendent power. The theological claim seems, on the surface, to contest the secular ontology of the subject.

Significantly, the charges against the cartoons were not blasphemy (*tajdīf*) but *isā'ah*—the latter means insult, harm, injury. Specifically, the cartoons were understood as efforts to coerce disbelief. And whereas Islam, according to Asad, offers no punishment for disbelief and in no way mandates belief, it opposes any efforts to coerce belief or disbelief. Belief itself is not a cognitive act, not even the "property" of a person, but part of an ongoing and embodied relation to God. So any attempt to coerce someone away from his or her belief is an effort to break a relation to a transcendence by which one is sustained. It is not, in these terms, a quarrel between beliefs or an attack on an idea, but an effort to coerce the break of a bond without which life is untenable. As Asad puts it, "what matters, finally, is belonging to a particular way of life in which the person does not own himself." The outrage against the cartoons articulates an objection to "something that disrupts a living relationship."

In light of this analysis, we can understand how, in the framework of the liberal legal imaginary, blasphemy is a charge that seeks to curtail free speech. The legal imaginary of liberal law, which protects free speech against blasphemy, makes the claim that the charge against the cartoons is blasphemy. This immediately makes the issue into one of whether or not free speech should be curtailed. On the other hand, to situate blasphemy— or in this case, *isā'ah*, insult, injury—in relation to way of life that is not based in self-ownership, but in an abiding and vital dispossession, changes the terms of the debate. It does not provide an immediate answer to how the question of prohibition or censorship should be legally decided, but shifts us into a mode of understanding that is not constrained by that juridical model. In other words, to understand blasphemy as an injury to a sustaining relation is to understand that we are dealing with a different conception of subjectivity and belonging than the one implied by self-ownership. (I am tempted to say that this mode of subjectivity functions as a critique of self-ownership within secular hegemony.) The public outcry against the cartoons is also a way of refusing and parochializing the specific property-driven ontology of the subject that has come to support the claim of free speech. In this case, to change the framework within which we seek to understand blasphemy makes it possible to see that what is at stake is not so much a question of whether speech should be free or prohibited as a way of conceiving a mode of living outside of self-identity and self-ownership. The cartoons are injurious not only because they fail to understand this way of life but also because they deploy the iconography of Muhammad to direct the viewer toward a repudiation of that way of life. To claim that someone or anyone can "own" the image is to seek recourse to a framework of property that is implicitly criticized by the living relation to the icon. So the critical question that emerges is whether ways of life that are based on dispossession in transcendence (and implicit critique of self-ownership) are legible and worthy of respect. It is then less a legal question than a broader question of the conditions of cohabitation for peoples whose fundamental conceptions of subjective life divide between those that accept established secular grounds and those at odds with secular presumptions of self-coincidence and property.

It would seem that we are being asked to understand this battle as one between, on the one hand, a presumptively secular framework tied to an ontology of the subject as self-owned and, on the other hand, a nonsecular framework that offers an ontology of the subject as dispossessed in transcendence. This explanation, however, asks us to assume that there is a certain generalized secular ontology of the subject, and that secularization has effectively succeeded in establishing that ontology within the parameters of law and politics. I have questions about whether the secular and secularization are as monolithic as this, but I will defer them in order to follow through with this argument. For if we accept that secularization is the way that religious traditions "live on" within postreligious domains, then we are not really talking about two different frameworks, secularism versus religion, but two forms of religious understanding, intertwined with one another in various modes of avowal and disavowal. Indeed, the binary framework crumbles further when we consider modes of secular criticism that take place in religious contexts (for example, the discourse of the current pope) as well as modes of religious reasoning that recur within secularism (for example, Protestant commitments to the distinction between public and private life that have become essential to modern liberalism).

Mahmood: Politics of the Icon

In some ways, Mahmood directs us toward the specificity of the relation to the icon in the Danish cartoon affair, launching a criticism of the presumption of state neutrality with respect to religion. Asserting the principle of state neutrality, understood as secular, some have argued that there ought to be no accommodation of religious sensitivities. In this way, the secular is understood as a practice of "abstention" in matters of religious sensitivity. According to Mahmood, secularism has never, in fact, been neutral with respect to matters of religion, but has been actively engaged in regulating and defining the domain of religion. In fact, the "neutral" law must be recast, in her view, as a productive and regulatory law, so that our very conceptions of religion now depend upon the stipulative force of neutrality. One way this works is by casting religion as a set of beliefs—and hence subscribing to a cognitive account of religion—but another way is through the privatization of religion, a strategy that separates state and religion by identifying public politics with the state and relegating religion to private life. How, she asks, do we reconcile freedom of religion with freedom of speech? Freedom of religion is understood as the freedom to assemble in private zones to practice religion, so "freedom" here is understood as a protection from coercion and prohibition. Indeed, that way of understanding freedom of religion relies upon and confirms a public/private distinction that cannot address some of the public forms that religion takes and some of the contemporary conflicts that call for understanding and adjudication.

So, one might reasonably ask, where does Mahmood stand on the question of legal redress for injuries sustained? It seems to me that there are two separate arguments at issue here, both of which have to be considered together in order to understand the complexity of her view.

On the one hand, Mahmood considers whether there are appropriate legal precedents that could serve the purpose of seeking redress for the injury caused by the blasphemy against Muhammad. Any effort to move in this direction would have to decide on an appropriate legal basis for making such a claim. There are three main arguments about these strategies in Mahmood's essay. If the ground for such a claim were that such depictions threaten public order, and that such depictions should be outlawed because of the threat to public order they create, then the claim would be strengthening a legal precedent (public order should be protected against incendiary representations) that has been used to fortify the rights of majorities over minorities. In this way, that legal move would strengthen a legal instrument that could very easily be used against religious minorities in European countries: "Muslims have come to be perceived as a threat to state security," which means that explicit representations of their faith may well fall within the category of incendiary depiction that threatens public order (indeed, the very presence of Muslims in Dutch and Belgian society, for instance, is considered such a "threat" according to several right-wing groups whose positions are becoming more, rather than less, mainstream). Mahmood thus counsels against this strategy.

A second strategy would be to show that the Danish cartoons could be conceived as hate speech and therefore subject to European hate speech laws. She considers as well that hate speech laws devised to protect racial minorities from discrimination tend to rely on a distinction between religious and racial minorities. This presupposition, however, fails to see that religious minorities can undergo racialization, becoming racial minorities. This failure to understand how the process of racialization works undermines the effort to distinguish in clear and timeless terms the difference between religion and race. And yet, even if a court were to accept the argument that, historically, Muslims have become racialized, would that be a good way to proceed? Mahmood does not come out in favor of this approach, but she seeks to show that the way in which religion and race are differentiated establishes the juridical domain as an instrument of certain embedded secular presumptions and, inevitably, a site for the reproduction of that secularism. For instance, religion is understood as a set of "beliefs" and even a matter of private choice and association. But what if the religion at issue is based less on cognitive belief than in embodied modes of existence that are bound up with certain texts and images? This raises the question of whether there ought to be, given the history and function of Western law, a legal solution to the problem at all.

Earlier, Mahmood considers that secular presumptions are at work in the way we think about pictures and subjects. In this extended and rich discussion, she points out that within Islam, the religious subject's relation to the representation of Muhammad constitutes a relation that is indissociable from one's own sense of self. The "self" at issue is not a discrete and bounded individual, but a relation to an animated image; the self has to be understood as a set of embodied and affective practices that are fundamentally bound up with certain images, icons, and imaginaries. In Mahmood's terms, "the power of an icon lies in its capacity to allow an individual (or a community) to find oneself in a structure that influences how one conducts oneself in this world… a form of relationality that binds the subject to an object or imaginary."[19] Now one might conclude that Mahmood is suggesting that blasphemy against the image of Muhammad is thus an injury to Muslim personhood, and that the law that seeks to distinguish between injurious conduct and incendiary expression misunderstands not only the ontology of personhood but also the character of the injury. The twin conceits of state neutrality with respect to religion are that (a) religion ought to be protected as a private issue and that (b) no religious beliefs should drive public law or policy. And yet, if religion becomes inextricably bound up with personhood, and injurious conduct against persons is legally proscribed, could not this new conception of the ontology of personhood mandate a change in legal reasoning and judgment?

Interestingly enough, Mahmood does not take this tack, but counsels against the domain of juridical redress as an appropriate and effective venue for taking up the challenge of the Danish cartoons. Instead, she uses the language of "moral injury" to distinguish the issue from the ways in which it is conceived by reigning legal vernaculars. Indeed, she is quite explicit about the policy implications of her analysis: "[T]he future of the Muslim minority in Europe depends not so much on how the law might be expanded to accommodate their concerns as on a larger transformation of the cultural and ethical sensibilities of the majority Judeo-Christian population that undergird the law." Moreover, this turn to the cultural and ethical domain is conditioned by an argument that the law is so pervasively secular that any effort to seek redress for injury through the law would strengthen the very instrument through which secularism asserts its hegemony and defines the proper domain of religion.

The final argument of her paper rests on several distinctions, quickly issued, that may not be as stable or clear as they appear. If the task is to change sensibilities, we need to know how that can be done. Of course, Mahmood is right to point out that the terms of existing law ought not to constrain our understanding of the cultural and ethical dimensions of this issue. On the other hand, is it right to understand law as radically distinct from questions of sensibility? After all, does law (civil rights law, for instance) not function on certain historical occasions to change sensibilities, to foster new parameters for equality and justice, including new sentiments, or are we being asked to understand "sensibilities" as definitionally extrajuridical? Are there not legal sensibilities at issue here?

This final call to change does not tell us in what way change might or should happen, which leads me to wonder whether we are being asked to take the foregoing analysis as precisely the kind of cultural and ethical intervention that is needed. If that is the case, several questions still emerge: do we understand the "cultural and ethical domain" to be radically distinct from law? and on what basis do ethics and culture constitute an alternative and separable domain or set of domains? Mahmood calls for "comparative dialogue" as well as a kind of "thinking" that happens in "unaccustomed ways," but what would be the institutional venues for these activities? Though these practices are considered distinct from "political action," are they for that reason not political strategies?

Mahmood specifies that we have to cleave judgment from description in the context of discussing religious fanaticism, presumably because our judgments tend to overwhelm our descriptions. And yet, how would we then return to the question of judgment after having made that initial separation? What form would some more fully informed judgment take? To enter into political action surely requires some kind of judgment about what is the case, and what should be the case. We have to consider whether politics is being allied with "law" or legal solution in this discussion, and what a politics might look like that did not model itself on juridical decision and action. When Mahmood makes the decision to turn away from law and politics, does she not inadvertently overlook the possibility of a politics, including a political judgment, that might not be constrained by legal norms or practice? Does "ethics" distinguish itself from politics as part of the effort to find an alternative to legal solutions in this matter? And does her argument now invest with neutrality the sphere of culture and ethics that has been wrested from law? Is this finally an apologia for anthropology itself? The final line invokes "the academy" as one of the few places where such tensions can be explored. Are we left, then, with academic exploration, comparative work, and dialogue as the cultural, if not culturalist, alternative to law and politics? This is a strange conclusion given how engaged with the politics of law the essay is, but perhaps we are meant to be persuaded that this is a domain from which we should all finally retreat. This final set of moves strikes me as curious, given that Mahmood has offered quite a few strong and well-argued political judgments throughout the essay: the pervasive secularism of European law; the misunderstanding of racialization; the widespread ignorance and hatred of Islam; the necessity to expose the secular production and deformation of religious practice. These are strong political positions. Even exposing the contradictions of secular law is clearly a strong critical move that seeks to combat a sustained and consequential hegemony within the law. Is Mahmood really operating to the side of politics and judgment? Can she give an account of the place of politics and judgment in her own analysis, indeed, in the argument she gives about why we should work to the side of both politics and judgment?

In a final coda, Mahmood raises the question of whether "critique" can take account of its own "disciplines of subjectivity, affective attachments, and subject-object relationality." At this point, it seems clear that the model for thinking about the Muslim relation to the image of Muhammad sustains certain analogies with the practice of critique itself. Both seem to be embodied and affective practices, modes of subjectivity that are bound up with their objects and, hence, relational. Is this a generalized account of subjectivity or one that pertains to specific kinds of practices of the self? This is not precisely a point pursued by Mahmood, but it does raise a question about the status of critique. In the end, she holds out for a notion of critique that relies on the suspension of the kind of closure characteristic of political action. So critique appears to be neither judgment nor action, but a certain invested, affected, way of thinking and living that is bound up with objects or, indeed, an imaginary, and this way of thinking—and what it thinks about—is not usual, not customary. Inasmuch as

secularism has established the domain of the usual and customary, there can be a critique of secularism that calls that taken-
for-grantedness into question. I take it that this would be part of
what Mahmood would accept as "critique."

In reading both Mahmood and Asad, one sometimes wonders
whether the problem is the "reputation" of critique as negative,
suspicious, taking religion as its object, differentiating itself from
dogma, where dogma is understood to be the presumptive characteristic of religion but not of secularism. But let us be clear that
critique is not the same as judgment, and that the formulation
of critique in Marx is not, as Wendy Brown has shown, without
its own history and legacy in religious metaphor and structure.[20]
Whereas Asad remarks that "the use and reception of criticism
depend on a variety of taken-for-granted understandings and
abilities, however temporary particular understandings and abilities turn out to be,"[21] Mahmood seems to hold out for a notion
of critique that is directed not only against the customary and
taken-for-granted understandings but also against those gener-
ated by secularism in particular.

Coda on Dutch Politics

It remains difficult to know under what conditions we understand speech to be a kind of action or conduct, and under
what conditions we understand it to be the free expression of
ideas. Films such as Geert Wilders's *Fitna* charge Islam with being a murderous religion, so there was some public debate in the
Netherlands in the Spring of 2008 over whether the film should
be shown, whether it had a "right" to be shown, and whether
state television should or should not be part of its showing. Would
the film cause social unrest (a consequentialist and securitarian
concern)? Would the film effectively discriminate against Muslim
minorities (a question of equal rights and, hence, of the range and
limit of hate speech law). It is possible to say that such films depict
violence, but also that they *do* violence, and, most peculiarly, they

do both in the name of freedom. To understand such a claim, we would have to know what kind of violence is depicted, what kind of violence is done (by the film), and what kind of violence emerged or will emerge in the response to the film: we have to be prepared to distinguish among kinds of violence if we want to locate violence in every dimension of this social scene, which would include the film's production, its content, and its reception. To use the same word "violence" for each dimension of the scene is not to assume that the same violence is at issue. Similarly, the term "freedom" has become highly contested in these debates. Is the freedom in free speech the same as the freedom to be protected from violence, or are these two different valences of freedom? Under what conditions does freedom of speech become freedom to hate? And how have these confusions sown discord within the European left?

For me, it has been particularly painful, for instance, to see how some members of the lesbian and gay community found themselves in a quandary, since freedom of expression and the opposition to censorship have clearly been cornerstones of the movement for decades. The movement for sexual freedom has required freedom of expression, and, in many places outside the Netherlands, censorship has inhibited the efforts of lesbian, gay, bisexual, trans, intersex, and queer people to publish, to assemble, to document and publicize their history, and to organize and express their desire. So it is quite understandable that there might be a strong group of sexual progressives who maintain that freedom of expression is essential to the movement, that the lesbian, gay, bi, trans, queer, intersex movement is not possible without freedom of expression and without recourse to freedom itself as a guiding value and norm. Of course, to posit such a principle of freedom does not answer the questions of whether and how that norm is to be reconciled with other norms, nor does it tell us precisely what is meant by "freedom."

We have to be clear about what we mean by freedom, since

from the beginning freedom has been, not the same as the liberty that belongs to the individual, but something socially conditioned and socially shared. No one person is free when others are not, since freedom is achieved as a consequence of a certain social and political organization of life. The queer movement, conceived transnationally, has also sought to fight homophobia, misogyny, and racism, and it has operated as part of an alliance with struggles against discrimination and hatreds of all kinds. The emergence of a queer politics was meant to confirm the importance of battling homophobia no matter what your identity was. But it was also a signal of the importance of alliance; an attunement to minoritization in its various forms; a struggle against precarious conditions, regardless of "identity"; and a battle against racism and social exclusion.

Of course there is also a now-entrenched tension between identity-based and alliance-based sexual minority politics, and my affiliation with "queer" is meant to affirm the politics of alliance across difference. Broadly put, a strong alliance on the left requires, minimally, a commitment to combating both racism and homophobia, combating both anti-immigrant politics and various forms of misogyny and induced poverty. Why would any of us be willing to participate in an alliance that does not keep all of these forms of discrimination clearly in mind, and that does not also attend to the matters of economic justice that afflict sexual minorities, women, and racial and religious minorities as well? So let us consider more carefully, then, how the politics of speech enters into this situation and how we might try to think about hate speech in light of a commitment to a left alliance that refuses to sacrifice one minority for another (which does not mean there may not be some serious antagonisms that remain essential to the articulation of this alliance). It is perhaps important to remember the importance of the critique of state coercion and state violence for a robust left political movement, even as we recognize that transnational economic institutions are responsible for differential poverty levels. Can we even think, though, about a politics of the speech act without noting how the state speaks, and what force it exercises when it speaks?

Clearly, the Netherlands has seen its share of violent speech acts. The wound that killed the Dutch filmmaker, Theo van Gogh, was literally a message that was violently thrust into his body.[22] And politicians across the political spectrum feel free to wage insulting discourse against Islam, as if Islam were a monolithic entity, as if their own murderous impulse belonged constitutively to the object of their hatred. Why is there a righteous defense of the political right to insult Muslim minorities at the same time that insults to the Dutch government, any critique of state coercion, constitutes an unacceptable assault on civilization, modernity, or reason itself? When this kind of split thinking happens, freedom of speech not only depends on protection by the state but empowers that state; this, in turn, leads to the situation in which speech against the state is effectively or implicitly censored. Hence, the freedom we think belongs to the individual is actually conferred by the state, so we misunderstand its origin and its meaning. This is also why, if we want to develop a critical conception of freedom of speech, it will have to be one that legitimates itself outside of state power, that is able to criticize state power as part of its free expression. We have to ask whether "relying on the state" leads to the "augmentation of state power." If Islam is figured as the religion or the name of the population who will do violence to Dutch civilizational values, then that gives the Dutch state a certain license to do violence to what seems to threaten its own values. That also logically means that "doing violence" becomes a Dutch value. We see the intensification of anti-immigrant activities, the base ideological implementation of the Civic Integration exam, the overt celebration of hateful speech of the so-called autochthonic Dutch against religious minorities as a sign of freedom itself.

The question is not whether hateful speech is part of free

speech, but rather, why has freedom in certain European contexts come to define itself as the freedom to hate? What does it mean when the notion of freedom has been twisted to ratify discrimination, xenophobia, racism, and nationalism?

The Dutch Civic Integration Examination was one case in point. In 2006, immigrants were required to take an examination that included the mandatory viewing of images of two gay men kissing as a way to test their "tolerance" and, hence, capacity to assimilate to Dutch liberalism.[23] Do I want this test administered in my name and for my benefit? Do I want the state to take up its defense of my sexual freedom in an effort to restrict immigration on racist grounds? What happens when seeking recourse to the protective actions of the state in turn augments and fortifies the state's own power, including its power to articulate a racist national identity? And what happens when lesbian and gay freedoms are instrumentalized to harass religious minorities or to ensure that new immigrants can be denied entry on religious, ethnic, or racial grounds? Under these circumstances, sexual progressives must become "critical" of the state that appears so enthusiastically to be supporting our freedoms. What precisely is it doing with our freedoms? And are we willing to have our claims to freedom instrumentalized for the purposes of a racist reproduction of Dutch national identity through restrictive and coercive immigration policies?

Let me make the point even more precisely, if I can. It is one thing for the state to value freedom of expression and to protect expression, but it is quite another for the state to be the agent who decides whose freedom of expression will be protected and whose will not. Under what conditions does the state decide that a minority is threatened by certain kinds of aggressive speech, and under what other conditions does the state decide that a minority must tolerate being targeted by aggressive speech as a sign that we live in a democracy that savors freedom of speech? Perhaps this is the new meaning for Dutch tolerance: you must tolerate the pain and abuse we will deal you, and that is the proof that you can "integrate" and become part of Dutch citizenship. We have to ask why the state gives free reign to racist speech at the same time that it demands respect for sexual minorities. Is the latter being played against the former? And what would happen if sexual and religious minorities refused to be pitted against each other in this way? What would happen if both of them turned against the nationalist and racist strategies of the state as a joint strategy?

If, following gay conservatives, we understand freedom as personal liberty and then base a politics on a libertarian notion of freedom, we sacrifice an important social dimension to the left understanding of freedom. If freedom belongs to the individual, then we can surely ask: which individuals are recognized as individuals? In other words, what *social forms of individuality* establish the recognizability of some persons as individuals and others not? If such an individual liberty exists only to the extent that it is protected by the state, then the state exercises its prerogative to protect in some instances and to withdraw all protection in others. Let's remember, then, that the libertarian notion of the individual corresponds to a certain version of state power and economic property, and, whereas in early versions of libertarianism the state is supposed to remain minimal (or privative) in order to maximize economic freedom, that is surely not the case in the present instance in which the state differentially protects rights depending on whether that protection suits its national aspirations, even its national self-understanding as "European," against the new immigrant communities from North Africa, Turkey, the Middle East, and Southeast Asia.

In the context in which the state makes use of liberties in this way (differentially exercises its prerogative to protect or retract individual liberties, decides who will count as an individual whose rights are worth protecting, and who will not), we have a different situation. In such a case, "freedom of speech" presupposes that there will be no open public criticism of the state or its inconsistent and racist actions (after all, the state is the protector and the adjudicator in this scene). This means, implicitly, that only those modes of freedom of expression will be protected that in turn protect the state, unless also protected is the open criticism of the state's racist speech. If the fortification of the state against established and new immigrant communities involves depriving them of freedom, questioning their own rights of assembly and expression, if it casts its own Muslim population as a threat to the value of freedom, then it protects one claim of freedom only through the intensification of unfreedom, through the augmentation of the state's own coercive mechanisms. If independent filmmaking is to remain a critical practice, separate from and willing to criticize state power, then one has to analyze closely the situation in which film becomes the cultural means through which the state's anti-immigrant practices are implemented and rationalized. The film industry then becomes the culture industry for the state, and it loses its standing as "independent" or, indeed, as "critical." Under these conditions, we lose the independence from state authority implied in the term "independent film," and that medium becomes a form of embedded reporting, taking on, even ratifying, the perspective of the state. As such, it becomes another visual instrument, like the cameras in Abu Ghraib, which stage and fortify the vicious embodied action of the civilizational mission, linking its propaganda against Islam with the torture and human rights violations in Iraq and Guantánamo.

Of course, the right to insult and the right to produce provocative art become rights that the state defends, but when it defends those rights differentially and for specific policy purposes, those rights become suspect. If those rights are to have legitimacy, they cannot be justified through recourse to their utility in rationalizing the deprivation of certain rights to religious practice and belief, in other words, certain rights of expression. There may be no legal way to "manage this risk," but that is no reason why this instrumentalization should not become the focus of critical analysis and political opposition. To understand when and where the claim of free speech is robust, we have to ask, "If we point this out, and maintain a critical and public relation to this particular prerogative of state power, is our speech still protected?" If it is still protected, then free speech is an active part of democratic contestations and political struggles. If it is not, we must militate against its restriction, differential application, and instrumentalization for nondemocratic ends.

If the prerequisites of a European polity (and this could be either the nation-state or the European Union) require either cultural homogeneity or a model of cultural pluralism, then, either way, the solution is figured as assimilation or integration into a set of cultural norms that are understood as internally already established, self-sufficient and self-standing. These norms are not considered changeable according to new demographic shifts, and they do not seek to respond to new populations and new claims to belonging. Indeed, if the core norms are already established, then one already knows what Dutch culture is, and one is closed to the idea that it may become something else, something different; indeed, one refuses the recognition that it already has become something different and that the change is, in fact, irreversible. When freedom of expression comes to mean "the freedom to express an unwillingness to undergo change in light of contact with cultural difference," then freedom of expression becomes the means through which a dogmatic and inflexible concept of culture becomes the precondition of citizenship itself. The state to which we appeal to protect the freedom of expression is the state that will close its doors to whomever it does not want to hear, whose speech is unwelcome within its borders. Within this framework, the freedom of personal expression, broadly construed, relies upon the suppression of a mobile and contestatory understanding of cultural difference. Such suppression makes clear how state violence invests in cultural homogeneity as it applies its exclusionary policies to rationalize coercive and discriminatory state policies toward Muslim immigrants.

When the acts of one member of a group or some small number of members of a group are taken to be the defining actions and beliefs of the group itself, then that is not only an unjustified generalization but also racism, and it must also be opposed. Surely, there is an ongoing clash or antagonism between those who feel that their values of sexual freedom or freedom of expression are threatened by some minority religious beliefs and ways of life, but these are differences to be worked out through cohabitation and struggle, through participation in public discourse, through cultural and educational projects, allowing modes of separateness to coincide with modes of belonging (and not trying to close the fissure between the two). These are surely better strategies than appealing to a state that makes use of the defense of "freedom" to reassert its national purity—its racist conception of culture—as the precondition of reason, modernity, and civilization, and to halt all public criticism of the way it polices its borders and patrols its minority populations. A racist discourse can recast itself as the necessary groundwork of morality, reformulating its own hatred as moral virtue. Some crucial part of freedom of speech involves "speaking out," which means, invariably, speaking out within specific scenes of address: speaking with and from and to one another. This implicit sociality in all address demands the recognition of freedom as a condition of social life, one that depends upon equality for its actualization. At stake is a rethinking of the processes of minoritization under new global conditions, asking what alliances are possible between religious, racial, and sexual minorities (when these "positions" are less identities than modes of living in relation to others and to guiding ideals). Then perhaps we can find constellations where the opposition to racism, to discrimination, to precarity, and to state violence remain the clear goals of political mobilization.

Endnotes

1. For an essay that stays within the juridical understanding of the events, see Robert Post, "Religion and Freedom of Speech: Portraits of Muhammad," in *Constellations* 14, no.1 (2007). Post's paper was also given as the Una's Lecture in 2007 at the University of California, Berkeley.

2. Cited from an unpublished earlier version of Talal Asad's "Free Speech, Blasphemy, and Secular Criticism," which was slightly revised after this response was written.

3. Judith Butler, "Non-Thinking in the Name of the Normative," in *Frames of War: When Is Life Grievable?* (London, 2009).

4. Talal Asad, *On Suicide Bombing* (New York, 2007), 20.

5. Raymond Williams, *Keywords* (New York, 1976), pp. 75–76.

6. Talal Asad, "Reflections on Blasphemy and Secular Criticism," in Hent de Vries, ed., *Religion Beyond a Concept* (New York, 2008), p. 586.

7. Cited from Asad, "Free Speech," unpublished version.

8. In Arendt's view, aesthetic judgment does not subsume existing particulars to already constituted categories, but seeks to open up new categorical schemes. See Hannah Arendt, *Lectures on Kant's Political Philosophy*, ed. Ronald Beiner (Chicago, 2002).

9. Talal Asad, "Free Speech, Blasphemy, and Secular Criticism," in this volume.

10. "An Interview with Gayatri Chakravorty Spivak," *Boundary 2* 20, no. 2 (1993): 24–50.

11. Walter Benjamin, "Goethe's Elective Affinities," in *Walter Benjamin: Selected Writings*, vol. 1, *1913–1926* (Cambridge, MA, 1996), p. 297.

12. See Walter Benjamin, "Theses on the Philosophy of History," thesis 17, in *Illuminations*, ed. Hannah Arendt, trans. Harry Zohn (New York, 1968), p. 263.

13. See Hermann Cohen, *Religion of Reason: Out of the Sources of Judaism*, trans. Simon Kaplan (Atlanta, 1995).

14. Perhaps most important, however, in tracing Foucault's Kantian genealogy is his *Introduction to Kant's Anthropology*, ed. Roberto Nigro, trans. Roberto Nigro and Kate Briggs (Boston, 2008). There Foucault points out a recurrent schism between the critical claim to transcendental reason and the study of man. The *anthropos* itself becomes undone through recourse to the idea of *Gemüt*, or inner sense, which might be compared to a notion of sensibility. See also Béatrice Han, *Foucault's Critical Project: Between the Transcendental and the Historical* (Stanford, 2002).

15. Michel Foucault, "What Is Enlightenment?" in *Ethics: Subjectivity and Truth*, ed. Paul Rabinow, trans. Robert Hurley and others (New York, 1997), pp. 303–20.

16. See Charles Hirschkind, *The Ethical Soundscape* (New York, 2006).

17   Michel Foucault, "What Is Critique?" in *The Politics of Truth*, ed. Sylvère Lotringer and Lysa Hochroth (New York, 1997), p. 25.

18   See Jody Greene, *The Trouble with Ownership: Literary Property and Authorial Liability in England, 1660–1730* (Philadelphia, 2005).

19   Saba Mahmood, "Religious Reason and Secular Affect: An Incommensurable Divide?" in this volume.

20   Wendy Brown, "The Sacred, the Secular, and the Profane: Charles Taylor and Karl Marx," a forthcoming volume of essays on Charles Taylor's *A Secular Age*, ed. C. Calhoun et al. (Cambridge, MA, 2009).

21   Cited from Asad, "Free Speech," unpublished version.

22   Theo van Gogh was a vocal libertarian Dutch filmmaker who was murdered in Amsterdam on 2 November 2004 by Mohammed Bouyeri, several months after the release of Van Gogh's film *Submission*. That film, made in cooperation with Ayaan Hirsi Ali, sought to show the abuse that Muslim women suffer by projecting verses from the Qur'an onto the nearly naked bodies of four Muslim women who tell their stories. The film was controversial, since it showed no concern for violence against women in other contexts, including secular households. But the reaction to the murder of Van Gogh, a strong libertarian, was universal outrage. The knife found in Van Gogh's body operated like a writing instrument, recalling the most graphic dimensions of Kafka's *In the Penal Colony*. Although Van Gogh was shot eight times with a gun, the knife became the symbolic instrument of death dealing when Bouyeri pinned a five-page statement, including Qur'anic verses, to Van Gogh's torso with a knife. The scene of the murder repeated the motif of attaching religious verse to the torso, suggesting that Van Gogh's film enacted a symbolic murder of Qur'an by making it responsible for violence against women's bodies, and yet Bouyeri's idiosyncratic and hideous use of the verse seemed eerily to confirm the murderous character of those words and the Qur'anic tradition. Unfortunately, the incident bolstered the worst fears and rampant ignorance about Islam, and displaced public attention from the question of new forms of Dutch intolerance toward new immigrants and how injury is understood within differing religious traditions to the question of why the demonization of Islam is supposedly perspicacious and righteous. A similar debate continues today in relation to the film *Fatwa* and whether it constitutes hate speech against religious minorities or ought to be regarded as free speech. Feminists and sexual progressives have been notoriously divided on these issues.

23   For an analysis of the Dutch Civic Integration Exam, see Eric Fassin, "Going Dutch," *Bidoun: Arts and Culture from the Middle East* 10 (Spring 2007, special issue *Technology*): pp. 62–63; see also my more extended discussion in "Sexual Politics, Torture, and Secular Time," in *Frames of War*. The examination was found unlawful in July 2008.

Talal Asad

Reply to Judith Butler

I CONTINUE THE CONVERSATION Judith Butler has initiated here about critique. In doing so, I set aside the many important points on which we agree. In what follows I try instead to persuade her, by clarification and elaboration of what I wrote, that we may also agree on other points.

I begin by endorsing Butler's insistence that intellectual inquiries into events such as the Danish cartoons scandal must go beyond the normative judicial framework to which the defenders of both "free speech" and "religious sensitivities" have addressed themselves. But I must say that her representation of what I try to do in my article isn't quite how I would put it. I am not concerned with "the meaning of the injury at issue" but with the assumptions of coherence that underlie what may be called the secular liberal interpretations of religious irruptions. When I look briefly at some conceptions in Islamic thought that overlap liberal ideas, I do so in order to see how the former can shed light on the latter (hence my extended discussion of "seduction," for example), not in order to seek to expand Western understandings of why so many Muslims felt injured. That is a praiseworthy undertaking, but it's not what I'm trying to do. My interest is not in what extralegal ways there may be "of acknowledging and repairing injury." I seek to explore the conceptual assumptions that underlie positions taken by so many secular liberals in discourses surrounding such events as the Danish cartoons scandal and the French head-scarf affair. More generally, my interest can be partly summed up in questions such as: How is the freedom of critique shaped? In what ways does its truthfulness connect to power? My debt here to Foucault is obvious. But there are other questions: Why does secularity invoke "maturity"? What happens to our political life when Christianity can claim "the secular" as its offspring, and secularity has the power to assign objects to the category "religion"?

Referring to something I wrote recently on violence,[1] Butler observes that "[b]y showing how normative dispositions (mainly secular and liberal) enter into stipulative claims (concerning objectionable violence and grievable death) that circumscribe the domain of 'understanding' contemporary cultural and military conflict, Asad facilitates a *critique* of this parochial and consequential circumscription of operative evaluative frameworks." I would put it differently: My effort aims at inciting the reader to consider the notions of objectionable violence and grievable death not in order to highlight the normative dispositions that have entered into evaluative frameworks but to examine what the concepts exclude and suppress, how they obscure their own indeterminacy and acquire their vitality. An examination of the binaries "objectionable/unobjectionable" violence and "grievable/ nongrievable" deaths problematizes the categories of *criticism* and *critique* as Butler uses them. I have often been asked to what moral or political end this effort at exploring and problematizing is directed (justice? compassion? truth?). My view is that there can be no abstract answer to this question because it is precisely the implications of things said and done in different circumstances that one tries to understand. I think one should be prepared for the fact that what one aims at in one's thinking may be less significant than where one ends up. By which I mean that in the process of thinking one should be open to ending up in unanticipated places—whether these produce satisfaction or desire, discomfort or horror.

Butler reproves me for confusing critique with criticism by explaining that "[c]riticism usually takes an object, and critique is concerned to identify the conditions of possibility under which a domain of objects appears." But does one have to choose between two mutually exclusive senses demanded by these definitions—the one of tediously finding fault,[2] the other of engaging in a high discourse about the conditions of knowledge? "The point of portraying and jeering at bad character types, at the boor, the surly, the buffoon, the harebrained enthusiast," writes Annette Baier, "is like the point of developing critical standards in appreciation of literature."[3] Making such discriminations is not only how everyday life is lived, it not only rests on the implicit understandings that make criticisms possible; it is also—in ways trivial and profound—how standards are recognized or proposed, and how disagreements can be expressed and debated. Thus fault finding (criticism?) can be linked to constructive appreciation, to affection—or to skepticism. On the other hand, identifying an object's conditions of possibility (critique) may be little more than an exercise in cruelty—or seduction. Notoriously, critique as the drive to truth may be motivated by delight in the sheer exercise of power over another (torture is only an extreme case of this), and conquest may indeed be critique's primary function. How should one compare these motivations of critique with those of fault finding? My question, then, is this: Can one engage in critique if one doesn't consider the activity of morally charged criticism as one of the conditions of possibility under which a domain of objects appears and is taken for granted—and if one doesn't attend to critique itself as the expression of a moral or religious attitude?

The postmodern theologian John Milbank finds in Augustine's *City of God* "the *original* possibility of critique that marks the western tradition, of which later Enlightenment versions are, in certain respects, abridgements and parodies."[4] Milbank's understanding of Augustinian critique straddles both the evaluation of objects in a sinful world *and* the identification of the conditions of possibility under which a domain of such objects appears. A religious psychology, including faith in divine grace, accounts for the possibilities of virtue and vice in worldly affairs and the objective limits of politics. The truthfulness of *this* critique is rooted explicitly in a theology that seeks to transcend the moral dispositionalism embraced by many secular and Christian liberals alike. I find this approach to critique interesting, but in my view what is called for is not locating the true *origin* of critique (whether in theology or in social science) but tracing its *genealogy* for our time—and thus engaging with what critique has now become in our secular world.

To show that an object's desirability or immovability or menace rests on contingent conditions is also in a sense to begin undermining its appearance. This possibility is both an opportunity and an anxiety for secular liberal politics because although critique *can* be destructive, for liberalism that destruction carries the promise of improved life but also the threat of chaos and continuous mess. I wonder, in this context, what exactly are Butler's anxieties and hopes?

So how should one understand critique (the laying bare of the conditions of possibility under which a domain of objects appears) when, in public life, it fails to bring listeners who belong to a different tradition around to the truth? My query here is not epistemological but political. It is not the secular claim to truth that worries me, but what critique may do to relationships with friends and fellow citizens with whom one deeply disagrees. Critique is no less violent than the law—and no more free. In short, I am puzzled as to why one should want to isolate and privilege "critique" as a way of apprehending truth. What does this do to the way one is asked to—and actually—lives?

Am I entirely wrong in suggesting that Foucault's conception of critique is founded on Kant's epistemological concerns, as Butler suggests? This is not the place to enter into a detailed discussion of Foucault's evolving views—nor was my essay on blasphemy. It is worth noting, however, that Foucault's early work, especially the *Archaeology of Knowledge,* clearly employs a Kantian concept of critique and that, even after his turn to Nietzsche, Kant's epistemological project is not abandoned; it is relocated genealogically. Thus in *Discipline and Punish* Foucault writes, "Beneath the increasing leniency of punishment, then, one may map a displacement of its point of application; and through this displacement, *a whole field of recent objects, a whole new system of truth* and a mass of roles hitherto unknown in the exercise of criminal justice."[5] This sense of critique is Kantian too, although here the practice of knowledge isn't simply limited by the way knowledge is organized, it is also productive of that organization. There seems to me another interesting shift evident in Foucault's lecture "What Is Critique?" where he comments on Kant's famous essay on the Enlightenment: "[I]t is characteristic that in this text on the Aufklärung Kant gives examples of the maintenance of mankind in immaturity, and consequently as examples of the points on which Aufklärung ought to lift this state of immaturity and turn men in some way into adults, precisely religion, law, and knowledge. *What Kant described as Aufklärung is indeed what I tried earlier to describe as critique,* as that critical attitude one sees appear as a specific attitude in the West from, I believe, what was historically the great process of the governmentalization of society."[6] Critique thus becomes for Foucault at once part of the historical emergence of governmentality and crucial to pulling mankind out of a state of immaturity in religion, law, and knowledge. Of course Foucault is fully aware of the Kantian distinction between limits and possibilities *interior* to the process of knowledge [critique] and limitations that are restrictions imposed by external authority [and rejected by Aufklärung], and he deals with it also in the discussion that follows the lecture.[7] What is interesting here is that for Foucault critique is an attitude, a way of living, because living as an adult requires thinking for oneself, rejecting external authority. This is true for Kant too, as Foucault points out. Butler may be right to cite Gayatry Spivak approvingly to the effect that "we can only subject to 'critique' that which we need in order to live." But the attitude Foucault identifies is precisely what defines this need: *In principle* there are no limits to critique, even if in practice everything cannot be interrogated at the same time. This is critique as enlightenment and maturity, not critique as an account of the limits internal to the process of knowledge. Its focus is not *what* we need to live but *how* we should live when we reach "adulthood."

Was critique also seen as essential to "the progress of mankind," to the need for humanity to move ever forward once it had attained *maturity*? I think so. The desire for social reform is as old as recorded history, but *this* notion of critique, integral to the individual's desire to govern himself, is not. It is not *any* form of criticism, not even the criticism employed in the eighteenth-century idea of progress as a finite process of education—that is enlightened. Critique of which Foucault speaks here articulates the desire (and the necessity) of continual, truthful self-reinvention—and perhaps encouragement of others to do the same—because that is how one demonstrates maturity to oneself. It is this that seems to me to constitute a heroic attitude, a particular view of subjectivity and its prime duty.

Of course Foucault's shift to genealogy and to governmentality transformed Kant's idea of critique through an attention to networks of power and knowledge, but he claims nevertheless that there is something that continues right through modern Western history, something essential to governmentality. And *that* something is critique regarded as a transcendent task. Butler rightly notes, when presenting her definitions of criticism and critique, that "although this latter seems like a Kantian definition, it is Kantianism that has been rewrought several times in the last few centuries with consequences for global politics within and outside the Euro-Atlantic." True, the concept of critique that Foucault inherited from Kant was reformulated over the last two centuries. But it must be stressed that that reformulation doesn't merely have an *intellectual* genealogy; it has gone through and been transformed by the changing experiences of revolutionary Europe, of the non-European world as it encountered the West's attempt to civilize it, and of today's capitalist consumer society. An account has yet to be given of the multiple materialities that have constructed our modern understanding of critique, of why critique now seems to some to be the indispensable way to truth and the essence of freedom.

It is often said that the nineteenth-century belief in unlimited progress was undermined in the first half of the twentieth century as European empires dissolved. But has a new domain of transcendent judgment—and the worldly actions issuing from that judgment—now given a new confidence to Euro-American believers in critique? I refer to human rights. The project to humanize the world calls on the North to assign rights (and emergency aid) to those in the South who need them, and to assume responsibility over their lives. After the Second World War the theory of sovereign state rights was formally qualified in the United Nations Charter—although ad hoc qualifications had appeared in the peace treaties after World War I. In the Universal Declaration of Human Rights, the absolute right to protection was shifted from states to individuals, with a consequent obligation placed on the Great Powers (now referred to by governments, journalists, and nongovernmental organizations [NGOs] as "the international community") to protect humans everywhere. The continuous exercise of criticism and critique by governments, journalists, and NGOs has been directed at ensuring that these rights and obligations are properly observed. International finger-wagging and many of the North's legal, financial, and military interventions are together designed to promote the conditions of possibility in which, ideally, everyone can govern themselves. These material interventions *are* critique; they are among the practices by which local appearances are dismantled and universal truth is encouraged, in which the South is taught, often coercively, the true meaning of *maturity.*

I hope that Butler will come to agree that, in practice, forms of criticism and critique are so intertwined that their vocabularies can't be neatly separated. The illocutionary acts they involve—questioning, judging, analyzing, accusing, defending, arguing, supporting, attacking, seducing, and so on—presuppose one another. Criticism/critique belongs to very disparate moral, political, and theological projects in the world. Butler is right to say that "every description is already committed to an evaluative framework" (although *framework* seems to me a too systematizing word), but I would urge her to go beyond this important recognition. We now need to address the following questions: What are the conditions of possibility under which the ethical and epistemological promise of "critique" emerges in contrast to the self-indulgence of "criticism"? When does intellectual "critique"—as against embodied practice—come to be regarded as the indispensable foundation of knowledge? How does power inform "critique," and how does "critique" sustain power? I hasten to add that these questions are intended not as a "criticism" of critique (because "critique has a bad reputation") but as a plea for a "critique" of critique, something that must begin with genealogy.

Endnotes

1   Talal Asad, *On Suicide Bombing* (New York, 2007). I have also dealt with the theme of acceptable and unacceptable violence in a forthcoming article: "Thinking About Terrorism and Just War," *Cambridge Review of International Affairs,* special issue: *Ethics and the Scholarship on War.*

2   Incidentally, I don't find Raymond Williams's entry on "criticism," in his *Keywords* (New York, 1976) as helpful as Butler does.

3   Annette Baier, "Moralism and Cruelty: Reflections on Hume and Kant," in *Moral Prejudices: Essays in Ethics* (Cambridge, MA, 1995).

4   John Milbank, *Theology and Social Theory* (Oxford, 1990), p. 389.

5   Michel Foucault, *Discipline and Punish* (New York, 1977), pp. 22–23; italics added.

6   Michel Foucault, "What Is Critique?" trans. Kevin Paul Geiman, in James Schmidt, ed., *What Is Enlightenment? Eighteenth-Century Answers and Twentieth-Century Questions* (Berkeley, 1996), pp. 386–87; italics added.

7   Michel Foucault, "Qu'est-ce que la critique? [Critique et Aufklärung] Compte rendu de la séance du 27 mai 1978," *Bulletin de la Société française de Philosophie* 84, no. 2 (1990): pp. 53 ff. Unfortunately, Geiman's translation, which I cited in my original essay for this volume (and to which Butler responds), omits the very interesting discussion that follows the lecture.

Saba Mahmood

Reply to Judith Butler

FIRST OF ALL, I would like to thank Judith Butler for taking the time
to engage with and comment on my essay. It seems to me that it
is only through a process of dialogue, commentary, and exchange
with interlocutors that one is able to both clarify and sharpen
one's arguments and to foreclose some common misunderstand-
ings of what one has said or written. It is in this spirit that I would
like to acknowledge the main points of convergence between us
and then move on to clarify what I think is a misreading of my
argument expressed toward the end of Butler's remarks.

I think it is important to state at the outset that we are in
agreement that the secular and the religious are not opposed but
intertwined both historically and conceptually such that it is impossible to inquire into one without engaging the other. I agree
with Butler that secularism neither entails a monolithic process
nor a single ontology of the subject. Having said this, however, it
is important to point out that there are certain modular arrangements and practices that have come to be identified with modern secularity (such as the ideological separation of church and
state or privatization of religion) that give secularism a certain
coherence and structure. It is a feature of modern secular power

to constantly regulate, identify, and demarcate what is properly religious from what is not (in which both state and nonstate institutions play a role). This does not mean, of course, that the ambition of secular power to coherence and regulation is stable or complete, but it does mean that its instability is contingently produced, the analysis of which requires attention to the particular concepts, institutions, and practices at play at a given historical conjuncture.

Let me turn to Butler's closing remarks on my essay, particularly where she accuses me of being a "culturalist," of abjuring politics and law in favor of ethics, thereby erroneously assuming that these are separable and autonomous domains. She asks if my turn to "the ethical" is in fact not an instance of the anthropological fetish for cross-cultural understanding that sidesteps questions of power and politics. This is somewhat surprising coming from Butler, whom I know to be a careful reader of my work. But let me state (and clarify) that I fully recognize that law, ethics, and politics are deeply intertwined, that it is impossible to engage with one without troubling the other. Note that the term *culture* is alien to my analytical vocabulary, and I do not evoke the familiar trope of "Islamic culture" here or elsewhere in my work. Islam for me is not a single "cultural formation" but, following Talal Asad, a discursive tradition whose practitioners struggle over what it means to live as a Muslim in this world, a struggle, furthermore, that unfolds in a field of power in which the historical development of "secular liberalism" commands considerable force and weight. The analysis I offer in this essay, for example, of the kind of moral injury at stake in the Danish cartoon affair, is one understanding among others of how a Muslim relates to the personage of Muhammad and is not coterminous with what might be called "Islamic culture." I suspect there are as many Muslims who would disagree with the model of relationship between Muhammad and pious Muslims that I outline in this essay as there are those who would concur with it.

My aim in outlining this specific relationship, and the particular kind of injury at stake, was not to provide an authoritative model for understanding why so many Muslims were upset by the Danish cartoons (that is, to provide a "cultural rationale" for their multifarious actions). Rather, I was puzzled at the time of the Danish cartoon controversy by the fact that so little attention was paid *both* in the Muslim and non-Muslim press to a conception of religiosity (expressed in folk devotional practices related to Muhammad) that cannot be easily subsumed into the language of identity politics so readily embraced by the critics and champions alike of the Danish cartoons. In this essay I wanted to think about the unintelligibility of this kind of religiosity as a diagnostic of the secular, what it tells us about the kind of moral and ethical claims that can be accommodated within a certain semiotic ideology of communication and meaning and within juridical language about freedom of speech and religion in European societies. The mode of analysis here is not culturalist. It aims instead to get at the terms of intelligibility through which one can even claim the space for tolerance in secular liberal discourse on the basis of the rights and protections extended to minority and majority communities of a nation-state.

As for how I view the relationship between the ethical, legal, and political domains, I think it is clear from the essay that my interest lies in showing the dense ethical commitments underlying the putatively neutral claims of the law (to mediate religious difference) and the political consequences that follow for Europe's Muslim minority. Butler reads my argument about the weight accorded to "public order" in European laws about free speech in terms of the prejudicial *use* to which they have been put: these laws, she states, have "been *used* to fortify the rights of majorities over minorities" (emphasis added). I want to note that for me the problem lies not so much in the *usage* (which presumes that the law can be put to a different *use*, one serving the interests of the minority instead of the majority) as in the structure of sensitivities, affects, and commitments (which I gloss as "ethical sensibilities") upon which the language of public order rests and to which it gives expression when deployed in the European Court of Human Rights decisions (or for that matter in Egyptian courts). To recognize the ethical underpinnings of the law is not to give causal primacy to the ethical, but to register the relationship between them, a relationship that is often ignored by legal practitioners, liberal political theorists, and, perhaps far more importantly for my argument, by European Muslims who want to seek protection within these laws.

As to how the ethical proclivities contained within the concept of "public order" are to be changed is of course a political question. Butler reads my call to European Muslims to work on the ethical register (instead of seeking protection within European laws or changing them) as a turn away from politics. Given the role civil rights legislation played in the transformation of majority attitudes toward the black minority in the United States, she asks how a political stance concerned with European minorities can turn away from using law as a weapon for social transformation. Let me clarify that it is neither my place nor intention to recommend a political program for European Muslims to follow. However, I do remain skeptical about the efficacy of European laws to effect political transformation in Europe (vis-à-vis the Muslim minority).

My reasons for skepticism are similar I believe to Butler's in *Excitable Speech,* where she warns against the double-edged character of state juridical power to adjudicate free speech and protect minorities against hate crimes and speech in the United States. While admitting that prosecution of hate speech may be unavoidable in some instances, Butler insists that the ability of the judiciary to adjudicate the injurious power of speech is saturated with and predicated upon the judiciary's unique power to enact violence through its own metonymic displacements and its redefinition of the meaning and context of what constitutes injurious speech. Analyzing the language used in two Supreme Court decisions in regard to hate crime (*R.A.V. v. City of St. Paul* [1992] and *Wisconsin v. Mitchell* [1993]), Butler argues that it is "necessary to distinguish between those kinds of violence that are the necessary conditions of the binding character of legal language, and those kinds which exploit that very necessity in order to redouble that injury in the service of injustice."[1] Similarly, at a different point in *Excitable Speech,* she is critical of activists and scholars who turn to the state to adjudicate civil liberties and instances of injurious speech (such as pornography). "What happens," she asks, "when we seek recourse to the state to regulate such speech? In particular, how is the regulatory power of the state enhanced through such an appeal?"[2] It is important to note that Butler here does not rule out all recourse to state power as a means for producing political change. Rather, her caution emanates from a careful reading of the characteristic ways in which the U.S. judiciary has sought to regulate hate speech in recent times. It is on the basis of these specific historical cases that she urges us to consider the discursive power acquired by the state when it is asked to pronounce on issues of injurious speech and civil liberty.

My reasons for cautioning against Muslim resort to Europe's hate speech laws and legally permissible restrictions on free speech are not that different from Butler's. As I argue, none of these laws are neutral mechanisms for mediating across different concepts and practices of religiosity but, as instruments of secular power, they demarcate and performatively produce normative notions of religion and religious subjectivity. This is especially true of the model of religiosity that I discuss in relation to Muhammad, with its attendant notions of iconicity and injury: how can this relationality be made commensurate with the kind of religiosity that is extended state protection under the right to religious liberty or free speech? Is the term *religion* in "the right to freedom of religion" clause simply neutral, capable of absorbing different conceptions of religious life and practice? Or do certain forms of religious difference have to be made "indifferent" in order to be given state protection? Can one draw parallels and distinctions between hate speech driven by racial prejudice and religious bias without reinscribing essentialist notions of religion and race or the power of the state to adjudicate such distinctions? What is erased in such a process of translation? What other avenues are imaginable to members of majority and minority populations of a nation-state to negotiate their differences despite the power asymmetry that characterizes this relation?

These are difficult questions that are political as much as they are ethical in nature; they entail both legal and extralegal sensibilities that are not easily parsed. To acknowledge and struggle with the ethical dimension of these questions is not to eschew politics but to recognize their mutual imbrication. More importantly, the point I wish to emphasize, one that echoes Butler's arguments elsewhere, is that these political and ethical questions cannot be collapsed into juridical discourse without risk of reducing political action to legal action and thereby reinscribing the state-sanctioned conceptions of religion and religious subjectivity. It is for this reason that I voice caution about the hasty turn to the law on the part of Muslims and non-Muslims to settle the score in the aftermath of the Danish cartoon controversy and instead urge perhaps a more difficult transformation of the social and ethical domains that is no doubt political in substance.

Does this position translate into a withdrawal into intellectual rumination instead of political action as Butler suggests? I do not think so. Both are necessary, but it would be a mistake to think that the labor involved in academic analysis, such as the writing of these essays or composing this response, is similiar to that involved in political action. While my intellectual endeavors are colored by my political views (and vice versa), to reduce one to the other is not to do justice to the distinct kinds of labor entailed in each praxis. Transforming the social and political circumstances in which today's Muslims live in Euro-America will require transformations of various kinds: transformations of their socio-economic power base, of their political and cultural legibility as European citizens (rather than imposter immigrants), and of their participation in civic and political life (in which law will no doubt play a role). All of these require action as much as judgment, but of a sort quite distinct from that undertaken in the practice of scholarly critique. The distinction I am making here is neither ontological nor epistemological, as Butler suggests, but consists in the distinct sort of material practices through which one imagines and creates a different world.

Here the question of norms is important. I am open to accepting Butler's argument that critique requires the shifting of normative assumptions that structure the possibility of knowledge. But I am always struck by the fact that academics are seldom moved to abandon their normative evaluative frameworks despite training and exposure to this kind of thought. Regardless of how many times I have presented this paper about competing understandings of the Danish cartoons with distinct political and ethical entailments, most of my academic audiences have a hard time putting aside their judgment that Muslims acted irrationally and their fear that this kind of religiosity, if allowed in the public sphere, would destroy the secular accomplishments of European society. My exercise in displacing strongly held views about the place of religion in public life is often met with deep suspicion and discomfort. (What is this woman trying to do?!) To decenter this intransigence, resistance, inertia, and suspicion I am afraid requires more than simply critique, and this is in part what I am trying to get at when I speak about the ethical register of sensible politics.

Let me close by way of an example. While civil rights legislation was no doubt transformative of racial politics in the United States, it should be noted that the activism of the civil rights movement extended beyond the strictly juridical domain. It also entailed performatively creating the space for the realization of black consciousness through a variety of collective and individual actions that were transformative of black and white sensibilities. While these actions were clearly linked to the eventual transformation of the laws regulating black-white relations, I find it interesting to think about the relation of the sensorial and ethical actions to the more crystallized demands for legal action: what were the cultural, ethical and sensible means by which the relations were affected and transformed?

Endnotes

[1]   Judith Butler, *Excitable Speech: A Politics of the Performative* (New York, 1997), p. 62.

[2]   Ibid., p. 77.

Contributors

TALAL ASAD is Distinguished Professor of Anthropology at City University of New York Graduate Center.

WENDY BROWN is Professor of Political Science at the University of California, Berkeley.

JUDITH BUTLER is Maxine Elliot Professor in the departments of Rhetoric and Comparative Literature at the University of California, Berkeley.

SABA MAHMOOD is Associate Professor of Anthropology at the University of California Berkeley.

CPSIA information can be obtained at www.ICGtesting.com
Printed in the USA
266846BV00002B/52/P